AN INTRODUCTION TO CONNECTICUT STATE AND LOCAL GOVERNMENT

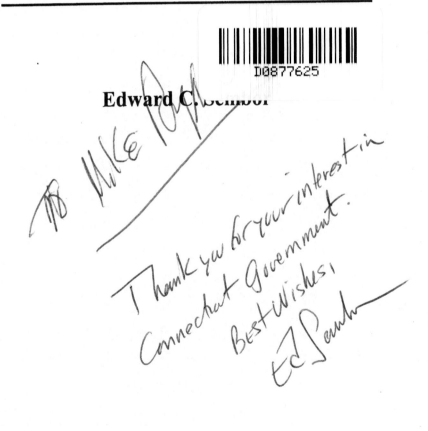

Edward C. Sembor

To Mike [signature] Thank you for your interest in Connecticut Government. Best Wishes, Ed Sembor

University Press of America,® Inc.
Lanham · Boulder · New York · Toronto · Oxford

Copyright © 2003 by
University Press of America,® Inc.
4501 Forbes Boulevard
Suite 200
Lanham, Maryland 20706
UPA Acquisitions Department (301) 459-3366

PO Box 317
Oxford
OX2 9RU, UK

ISBN 0-7618-2626-2 (clothbound : alk. ppr.)
ISBN 0-7618-2627-0 (paperback : alk. ppr.)

To

Lynn Marie
Kathryn Elizabeth
and
Jacqueline Lois

for their patience and love.

TABLE OF CONTENTS

LIST OF TABLES

LIST OF FIGURES

PREFACE

It seems that I have always been interested in local government and public issues. As a youngster, I enjoyed working for local political candidates at election time. As a college senior at Fairfield University, I served as an intern in Connecticut's General Assembly. After earning two graduate degrees in political science from Fordham University, my first job out of graduate school was as an analyst at the Office of Management and Budget in New York City under Mayor Edward Koch. Later, I accepted a position in a similar capacity for the Town of West Hartford, Connecticut. I eventually came to work at the Institute of Public Service at the University of Connecticut which is a unit of the College of Continuing Studies. The Institute provides training and educational program development for state and local public officials.

At the University of Connecticut, Professor John Rourke knew of the work I was doing in local government at the Institute and as department head, asked me if I would teach the course on Connecticut State and Municipal Politics. The writing of this textbook was prompted by teaching that course several times. As I began to prepare for the course and gather materials that might be interesting for undergraduates, I found that there was very little available in terms of current academic materials appropriate for a college level political science class on Connecticut politics and government. There were some classic studies by Duane Lockard, a well respected authority in the field, but they had become dated. There were other, more recent monographs concerning specific areas of government, but they too were becoming dated and lacked a truly comprehensive perspective. I made it a point to bring a copy of *The Hartford Courant*, a widely circulated Connecticut newspaper to each class for discussion on pertinent political developments at the state and local level.

I began to gather these books, articles, and publications together with the thought that someday I would attempt to consolidate and synthesize them into a coherent textbook which would provide an introductory but comprehensive overview of government and politics at the state and local level in Connecticut. The textbook which follows is my humble attempt at that task. Chapter One provides an overview of some of the current issues that have provided the context in which government in Connecticut operates. It concludes with a discussion of political culture in Connecticut and the challenges of defining it. Chapter Two discusses the historical evolution of the Connecticut constitution. Chapter Three reviews the state of political parties within the state, campaign finance, and running for political office. In Chapter Four, the legislative process and the role of lobbies is discussed. The role of the state Governor and other statewide constitutional officers is the focus of Chapter Five. Chapter Six provides an overview of the Judicial Branch. In Chapter Seven, forms of local government and other municipal institutions and actors are discussed. The book ends with Chapter Eight which provides a discussion of the state of democracy in Connecticut.

ACKNOWLEDGEMENTS

In this book I have tried to provide a comprehensive overview of some of the political actors, institutions and processes that are found in the state of Connecticut but I have had much help in the effort. I remain grateful to Professor Rourke for giving me the opportunity to teach and thus learn much more about some of the details of political life in Connecticut. For the students who have sat in my Connecticut State and Municipal Politics and State and Local Government classes over the last few years, I wish to thank them for their questions, comments and enthusiasm for learning. I would like to thank in particular two outstanding public officials who, through their ideas, comments and suggestions have made this effort a far better one than it might have been. They are Denise Merrill, Connecticut State Representative and Jason Jakubowski councilman on the New Britain Common Council. David Y. Miller, Associate Dean and Associate Professor with the Graduate School of Public and International Affairs at the University of Pittsburgh read an early version of this effort and was kind to raise some very constructive questions and offer several well aimed suggestions. Kay M. Warren of BarDan Associates, did an outstanding job in preparing the camera-ready copy of the manuscript. Finally, I would like to thank my father, Edward C. Sembor, Sr., a retired managing editor for technical communications at a major business equipment company. His review of the grammar, syntax and punctuation greatly contributed to the overall improvement of the text. This being said, I alone assume full responsibility for any error of omission or commission that may be found within.

ECS

Chapter 1

CONNECTICUT POLITICS
AND GOVERNMENT IN CONTEXT

As Connecticut starts on her fourth century of self-government, un-limited possibilities for achievement, both material and spiritual, lie ahead. The people of this state have met heroically the enemies of the republic without, and they are alert to more subtle dangers from within. Of these it has been said that the greatest menace to freedom is an inert people. . .

· Today, we of Connecticut are going forward to meet the problems and opportunities of our state in the spirit of practical idealism summed up in the terse speech of our first Connecticut Yankee, Thomas Hooker, "As God has given us liberty, let us take it. "

By James Daugherty and Philip E. Curtis in
An Outline of Government in Connecticut. 1949[1]

    The above were the concluding words of James Daugherty who wrote a small booklet about Connecticut's government which was widely distributed in the state nearly 60 years ago. The world, the nation and the state have become much more complex six decades later, yet the message of these words still seems to resonate in 2002. Especially poignant since September 11, 2001, is his statement of how the people of the state, "have met heroically the enemies of the republic without, and they are alert to more subtle dangers from within." If nothing else, Daugherty's words serve to remind us that now, in 2003, Connecticut is more than midway through her fourth century of self-government.

    Duane Lockard, a scholar of state politics, has said that, "For all their formal comparability, the fifty states are essentially very different."[2]

    That is essentially the main reason that every state, on its own, is worthy of study. Connecticut's political history, which predates the American Revolution by over one hundred years, can certainly be called one of the oldest among the fifty states. Like the other forty-nine, as the state embarks upon the new century, it faces political concerns, issues and opportunities that will require the full attention of its public officials and those responsible for running the state and local governments. Political scientist Harold Lasswell once discussed politics as the study of influence and who gets what, when and how.[3] While the 50 states of America share many of same structures of representative democratic government, this, "land of steady habits," as Connecticut is sometimes called, has its own unique set of social, economic and political issues that have driven public policy and which will continue to help shape and influence the state's political character. By taking a closer look at some of Connecticut's political actors and institutions, the processes that they work through and the outcomes that result, we may come to a better understanding of how Connecticut government as a system functions and who gets what, when and how within the state.

As the State of Connecticut came to the end of the 20th century and began the 21st, casual observers might have noted that, upon reflection, there were several significant developments within government that had presented themselves. What follows is a brief summary that touches upon some of the more significant and recent developments which have had political ramifications and are sure to influence the future.

REDISTRICTING

Perhaps the most significant political development for Connecticut as a state has been the shift in the U.S. population since the 1990 census. While Connecticut's population did grow slightly over the last decade, from 3,287,116 to 3,405,565 or about 3.6 percent, the growth was minor compared to that of the Sunbelt and the Mountain states and not enough growth to prevent the loss of one congressional seat.[4] The result, which many had long feared, was the loss of one of Connecticut's seats in the U.S. House of Representatives, reducing Connecticut's representation in the lower house of Congress from six to five. What made this development especially interesting was that at the beginning of the new century, Connecticut's six representatives were evenly divided among three Democrats and three Republicans.

Once the numbers came in, the politically challenging and contentious task of redistricting began. The State Joint Reapportionment Commission was composed of eight members of the General Assembly, four Democrats and four Republicans. The Commission began holding its hearings in late June, 2001. By law, this commission had until September 15 to come up with a redistricting plan. If it could not, then the eight commission members would appoint a ninth member and the deadline would be extended to November 30.[5] If no plan could be agreed to by then, the Connecticut Supreme Court would have until February 15 to devise or cause to be devised a plan. This nearly happened. The Joint Reapportionment Commission missed not only the first, but the second deadline as well and for the first time in Connecticut history, the redistricting plan went to the Supreme Court. Many state law makers favored keeping the redistricting issue a legislative matter and a petition referring the duty of planning back to the commission was filed with the court. The Supreme Court granted the Legislature a short extension and on December 21, the Commission unanimously voted out a plan. The end result was a new electoral configuration in which the Fifth and the Sixth Congressional Districts, represented by congressional veterans Republican Nancy Johnson and Democrat James Maloney, respectively, were combined into a new Fifth Congressional District. The race in this redrawn district promised to be a ferocious political battle in the November 2002 Congressional elections. By the final tally, Johnson won a race that was not as close as predicted, but, with her campaign expenses exceeding $3 million, it will surely be remembered as one of Connecticut's most expensive congressional contests.[6]

Connecticut House and Senate districts were also redrawn to reflect the new census numbers. Some voters were shifted into other towns, such as a section from the Town of South Windsor to the 11th District of East Hartford. Population shifts along some shoreline towns led to the formation of a new house district composed of Old Saybrook. Lyme, Old Lyme and part of Westbrook.[7] For the first time in thirty years, the Town of Southington has one State Senator.[8] The new districts that resulted from population shifts caused new electoral configurations throughout the state. Some Connecticut politicians saw this positively, others did not. Tom Swan, Executive Director of the Connecticut Citizens Action Group in Hartford, thought some of the new boundaries were drawn to protect political careers, saying, "I did find the shape of the New Britain districts to be very weird."[9]

TAXATION

The 1992 estimate for Connecticut's budget was a shortfall of $2.4 billion. While opinions for this fiscal predicament vary, Republicans claimed that Democrat imposed taxes on businesses that were punitive drove off revenue sources and that the state's spending during the 1980s was excessive. Sales taxes were high as well as were capital gains taxes and taxes on dividends.[10] Connecticut was clearly headed for fiscal disaster.

In 1991, under the newly elected, independent governor Lowell P. Weicker, Jr., a former Republican U.S. Senator, a personal income tax was narrowly passed as part of an overall tax restructuring effort, making Connecticut the 41st state to have such a tax and giving the state, in the opinion of many, a more stable and progressive source of revenue. While there may be the perception by some that the middle class pays the highest proportion of their taxes to the state's income tax, it is the wealthiest in Connecticut who pay the greatest share of the income tax. The five towns contributing the greatest share to this tax are New Canaan, Greenwich, Weston, Darien, and Westport, all within Fairfield County, Connecticut's wealthiest.[11] The total revenue generated by the personal income tax was $3,820.8 million in fiscal year 1998-99, accounting for 36 percent of the state's total revenue.[12]

The later 1990s saw the state enjoying the status of having revenue surpluses. The 2002 state budget however, largely due to lower tax collections, higher unemployment, and greater consumer uncertainty due to the impact of the terrorist attacks of 9/11 faced a deficit of several hundred million dollars, leaving John Rowland, a popular governor with some very tough choices. At the local level, with the wallets of homeowners continually stretched to provide for local services, property tax reform continued to be a challenge facing state and local officials. About 65 percent of municipal revenue in Connecticut comes from local property taxes.[13] The Connecticut Conference of Municipalities has argued that this represents an over reliance of the property tax in funding municipal services. The average effective tax property tax rate, a rate used to compare the tax burden between municipalities, in fiscal year 1999-2000 was greater than at any point in the last decade.[14]

HEALTH CARE

A very significant development within the healthcare area in Connecticut has been the HUSKY Plan. In October of 1997, Governor Rowland signed into law a health care plan for Connecticut children up to age 19 who do not have health insurance. This program is supported by state and federal funds and is administered by the Department of Social Services. Called HUSKY, which stands for Healthcare for Uninsured Kids and Youth, the plan includes several components. HUSKY Part A includes services for children under the Medicaid program. HUSKY Part B is healthcare for children with higher incomes. HUSKY Plus is a program for children with intensive physical or behavioral health needs.[15] In another area, in early 1999, the Office of Health Care Access, the state agency that ensures that the citizens of Connecticut have access to quality health care, was awarded a three year, $664,000 grant from the Robert Wood Johnson Foundation for the ACHIEVE (A Connecticut Healthcare Initiative for Expansion, Value and Efficiency) program.[16]

In his budget for 2000-01, Governor Rowland appropriated $8.2 million from state surplus to expand and realign the services provided by the Department of Mental Health and Addiction Services.[17] In 2000, Attorney Richard Blumenthal filed a lawsuit against four of Connecticut's largest HMOs. The suit accused them of using guidelines that arbitrarily denied members coverage, denying patients access to prescription drugs and failing to pay physicians and hospitals in a timely manner.[18]

While one of the states most urgent problems in the health care area remains the shortage of qualified health care professionals in hospitals and nursing home facilities, in other areas of health, there have been some very positive developments.[19] The infant mortality rate has decreased from 17.2 deaths per 1,000 live births in 1970 to 6.1 in 1999. The teenage birth rate declined during the 1990s. There was a decrease in the percentage of the state's population without health care insurance.[20] As of 1998, the age-adjusted mortality rate for all causes of death fell to its lowest point since 1980; death rates decreased for HIV infection, heart disease, cancer and suicide; and the median age of death increased for both men and women.[21]

TRANSPORTATION

According to a report by Michael K. Gallis, entitled, *Connecticut Strategic Economic Framework: Defining the Issues, Relationships and Resources Necessary to Compete in a Global Economy*, New England has become the "new Atlantic triangle" with the angles being New York City, Albany and Boston. Connecticut lies within this triangle, but risks being left out of any economic benefits if it fails to improve its transportation system.[22]

Traveling on Interstate 95 in southwestern Connecticut, it is not difficult to understand why many think the state's roads are overcrowded and congested. Between 1988 and 1998 total travel in the state grew from

71.2 to 79.9 million vehicle miles, this measure occurring while the state was loosing population. According to economists Heffley and Lanza, "Connecticut's 160 residents per mile of road in 1998 was more than double the 1997 U.S. average of 68."[23]

This issue has been taken seriously. Speaker of the House, Moira Lyons in the fall of 2000 convened a statewide transportation summit to review transportation issues and problems. Out of this summit came a 15-member Connecticut Transportation Strategy Board, composed of public and private sector members. Key areas of focus for this Board are: linking transportation planning, economic development and quality of life; the connectivity among different forms of transportation and the creation of objective criteria to evaluate transportation projects for funding.[24]

In the 2000-01 the Department of Transportation accomplished $280.2 million worth of construction, including reconstruction of portions of the interstate system, improvement at Bradley International Airport, state road reconstruction, rehabilitation of bridges and rehabilitation and resurfacing of roads.[25]

PARKS

Connecticut maintains 182,220 acres of state parks forests which offer swimming, boating, fishing, hiking, hunting and picnic facilities.[26] In 1997, the Department of Environmental Protection announced a $114 million statewide State Park Infrastructure Improvement Initiative. Known as the "2010 Plan," these improvements will take place over the following 12 years.[27] In fiscal year 1999, there were considerable improvements and renovations in this area; an $812,000 improvement project was begun at the Indian Well State Park, handicapped accessible beach bathhouses and first aid lifeguard offices were opened at Sherwood Island State Park and a $500,000 facelift was given to the Heublein Tower at Talcott Mountain State Park.[28]

EDUCATION

In comparison to all the states, Connecticut ranks fourth in terms of average per pupil educational expenditures.[29] In 1999-2000, a total of $5.2 billion was spent on elementary and secondary public school education. About 53 percent of this total came from local sources of revenue.[30] In comparison to other states, Connecticut has enjoyed some impressive rankings. In terms of reading and math proficiency for fourth graders, Connecticut ranked first among all fifty states. Connecticut ranked fifth nationally in combined math and verbal SAT scores with an average score of 1019 and with 80 percent of high school graduates taking the test.[31] The high school drop out rate improved to its best record since 1970. It declined from 4.7 in 1991-92 to 3.0 in 1999-2000.[32] A national report, The "Quality Counts 2001 Report," ranks Connecticut high in terms of student achievement, standards and accountability, teacher quality, and school climate. Yet it ranked considerably lower in terms of balancing school spending between wealthier and poorer school districts.[33] Most notably, cities like Hartford, despite a state takeover of its school system, continue to be challenged in terms of overall ranking.

CASINO GAMBLING

Connecticut now is the home of one of the biggest gambling casinos in the world. The Foxwoods Resort Casino, in Ledyard, was opened in 1992 by the Native American Mashantucket Pequot tribe. A second casino, The Mohegan Sun Casino, opened in 1996. Together, the two casinos provide about 20,000 jobs and generate extra earnings of more than $1.25 billion per year in New London County.[34] As part of the agreement between the state and the Mashantucket Pequot Tribe, Connecticut receives 25 percent of the net "win" from the casino's slot machines, but not less than $100 million annually.[35] In fiscal year 1999, revenue coming into the state's budget from Indian gaming reached over $288 million, representing just under 3 percent of the total General Fund revenues.[36]

The economic benefits to the state from the casinos have also come with challenges. The surrounding towns have had to endure more traffic congestion and resulting burdens from casino visitors. In August of 2000, *The Hartford Courant* reported that the number of compulsive gamblers in state-funded treatment programs had steadily increased from 50 in 1993 to 425 in 1999.[37] The Connecticut Council on Problem Gambling reported in 2000 that about 47 percent of those calling their telephone hotline were women.[38]

SOCIAL HEALTH

Connecticut is the only state in America that annually reports on the state of its social health. Through a collaborative effort by the Connecticut General Assembly and the William Caspar Graustein Memorial Fund, data on eleven indicators is collected and summarized every year by the Fordham Institute for Innovation in Social Policy to develop an indication of the quality of life in the state. The result is an index number based upon a total possible score of 100. These indicators include: Infant Mortality, Child Abuse, Youth Suicide, High School Dropouts, Teenage Births, Unemployment, Average Weekly Wages, Health Care Costs, Violent Crime, Affordable Housing and Income Variation. With data being reported since 1970, The 2001 Social State of Connecticut Report reflects data as of 1999. The index score for 1999, of 60 out of a possible 100 overall, reflects five consecutive years of improvement since 1994 which had the worst index score of 41. Some indicators are notably very positive. The teenage birth-rate has shown decline, unemployment has remained comparatively low, and per capita income remains the highest in the country. On the down side, the child abuse rate is the highest since the reporting started. In 1999 the rate of referred cases for child abuse was more than 49 per 1,000 Connecticut children under 18. Income inequality continued to increase, with the gap between the poorest county and wealthiest county again showing growth.[39]

During the 1990s there was an overall decline in criminal activity in Connecticut. Murder, rape, robbery and aggravated assault in the state declined in 1999.[40] The Connecticut Crime Rate Index is a compilation of crimes reported for the entire state developed by the state's Department of Public Safety. The index records the total number of index offenses which include: murder, rape, robbery, aggravated assault, burglary, larceny and motor vehicle theft. In 1991 the crime rate index score, which is based upon the total number of crimes per 100,000 persons was 5,378.70. By 2000, this score had dropped to 3,238.76.[41]

TRUST IN GOVERNMENT

With the headline grabbing scandal involving political campaign kickbacks surrounding the State Treasurer's Office, the citizens of Connecticut have, in the last several years, seen public officials involved in a number of illegal activities. Former state treasurer Paul J. Silvester pleaded guilty to federal charges of racketeering and laundering money in September, 1999.[42] The treasurer would invest state pension funds with investment management companies and then have the companies direct finder's fees, jobs or contracts to specific individuals.[43] The plights of the mayors of two of Connecticut's largest cities added to the sense of ethical collapse in some regions of the state. In the case of Waterbury, former Mayor Giordano faces federal criminal charges of having used a regulated communication device to entice a minor with sex.[44] In the case of Bridgeport, a circle of administrators, advisors and friends of Mayor Ganim have admitted to guilt in receiving kickbacks, mail fraud and racketeering on lucrative city contracts. The mayor, who has steadfastly maintained his innocence, himself was indicted for accepting money and gifts in exchange for city contracts.[45]

. In the late 1990s the state's sheriff's system came under strong criticism. The last remnant of Connecticut's abolished county government, sheriffs were largely responsible for serving civil process, prisoner transport and courtroom security. The rape of a female prisoner while being transported in a sheriff's van by other prisoners, the hiring of convicted felons as deputy sheriffs and the arrest of a sheriff for embezzlement led the governor to call for a disbanding of the sheriff system and caused the General Assembly to call a statewide referendum for a Constitutional Amendment eliminating county sheriffs.[46] In November of 2000, by popular vote, the 334 year old sheriff system passed into history.

POLITICAL CULTURE

Political culture broadly defined may be considered as the set of beliefs and values that the people of a nation respect and enjoy as individuals and as citizens within a structure of government. These beliefs and values are expected to be reflected in the operation of their government. In America, whether someone may think of themselves as liberal or conservative, Democrat, Republican, independent or otherwise, there appears to be a general belief in the values of justice for all, for equal individual rights and freedoms, and for democratically elected, representative government, accountable to the people.

Connecticut has been known by many different names through its history, some of which may hint at the nature of its political culture. The Constitution State, the Nutmeg State, the Provision State and the Land of Steady Habits all may provide some insight as to how the people of Connecticut have considered themselves. Connecticut as the Constitution state describes its very seminal influence, through the creation of the Fundamental Orders, on the importance of the concept of commonwealth and for a written and limited structure of government. Connecticut, as the Nutmeg state, recalls the early inclination of Connecticut citizens to move on from their Puritan origins and take on the role of independent, Yankee entrepreneur. Connecticut as the Provision State brings to mind the willingness that the state has demonstrated in working hard in stocking America's arsenal in times of war and conflict since the American Revolution. The Land of Steady Habits speaks to the image of Connecticut as a fair, even-handed and stable state, capable of change, but only after careful consideration of all the options.

In 1991, the Connecticut Humanities Council and Connecticut Public Television produced an insightful video about Connecticut's identity entitled, *Between Boston and New York*. Throughout the video, various commentators attempt to pin down some significant aspects of Connecticut's character. What the viewer ultimately finds is that Connecticut means many different things to many different people. It is the rural town green with the white clapboard church; it is the busy city streets of New Haven and Hartford; it is the land of the genteel, gentleman farmer; it is the home of the urban poor struggling to survive; it is the home of strict Puritanism and the birthplace of the shrewd, entrepreneurial Yankee. A very revealing point made in the video, in terms of Connecticut's political culture, is that with 169 towns and no county government to bind them, there is little that the towns have in common, except a strong sense of localism. It may be that, as the commentator of the video put it, "Our identity is our lack of identity."[47]

Daniel Elazar defines political culture as a pattern of orientation to political action. Further, it is deeply embedded within the particular historical experiences of a people.[48] As a nation, American political culture has developed within a dynamic tension between two different perspectives of what our orientation to political action should be. These are the concepts of liberalism, with its keen respect for individual rights and republicanism, with its obligation for citizens to participate in self-government.[49] James Morone has referred to this dynamic interplay of these two contending concepts as the democratic wish, "the recurring American ideology of revolution and reform."[50] Connecticut, with its history of local town meeting government, well demonstrates its republican roots. It also has shown throughout its history an ever expanding sensitivity to individual rights, from disestablishing the Congregational Church as the state sanctioned religion in 1818 to its present concern over public school desegregation.

According to Elazar, three distinct political cultures inhabit the states of America. These are called the individualistic, the moralistic and the traditional political cultures. Under the individualistic culture, politics may be viewed as business. Here the pursuit of private goals and individual freedoms is most prominent and politics is left up to those who are good at it. Under the moralistic culture, there is a strong Puritan influence and the emphasis is on establishing a good society where all citizens should participate and the active promotion of the common good is pursued. The traditionalistic culture is largely based upon a hierarchical social structure and the maintenance of the existing order. Here, political participation is seen as the privilege of an elite.[51] Elazar cautions that political culture is dynamic and that no one state may be completely placed within one category. Yet it is likely that a specific political culture will be dominant within a state due to its own unique history.

Connecticut, according to Elazar's scheme, is dominantly individualistic with a strong moralistic influence. Does this seem to fit the Nutmeg State? The early Puritan influence supplied by the Reverend Thomas Hooker and the Fundamental Orders and the still strong tradition of town meeting government are important in understanding the moralistic influence. Connecticut's rapid evolution into a state fully embracing the industrial revolution and its more recent history as a manufacturing center for the aviation industries and as an insurance and financial services center provides support for a strong sense of individual advancement and entrepreneurship.

Political researchers Erickson, McIver and Wright have found that in the United States, geographic location plays an important role in the formation of political opinion. In a national study, they found that a person's state of residence is an important predictor of partisan and ideological identification. Compared to other states at the time of their study, which was completed in the 1980s, Connecticut appeared more ideologically liberal and more politically Republican.[52] If one is willing to consider Connecticut in terms of sharing a regional cultural identity, a study by Moon, Pierce and Lovrich in 2001 might provide some insight. Their study compared political cultures of cities in specific regions of the United States. They examined the variables of social trust, self-esteem and liberalism as dimensions of political culture. As one of several states within the Northeast, it can be argued that Connecticut would share to some degree the characteristics of other states in the same region and thus some inferences about its political culture might be drawn. On the dimension of social trust, which was measured as community expectations of cooperation and honest behavior of community members, the Northeast had higher mean scores than all other regions except the South. On the dimension of self-esteem, or how individuals view their own worth and how they think others view their worth, the Northeast scored higher than all other regions except the Rockies. On the dimension of liberalism, which was conceptualized as supporting social issues that favored those parts of society normally viewed as having less power, the Northeast scored higher than all other regions except the Pacific.[53]

    Scholar of Connecticut politics, Clyde D. McKee, Jr., states that Connecticut's political culture is complex and a challenging one to understand primarily because of four factors. These are, "strong influences from colonial heritage, particularly at the local level; great diversity among religions, racial and ethnic groups; significant differences in personal wealth and economic advantage and continuous private and public adjustments to Connecticut's loss of old, labor intensive non-defense-related industries."[54] Connecticut still is known as, "the land of steady habits," but perhaps its most significant characteristic has been the ability of its diverse people to adjust, adapt and accept change.

    While Connecticut may be characterized a liberal state ideologically, more partisan change cannot be unexpected, especially for such an individualistic state. In 2002, while John Rowland remained a popular Republican governor, the state had two very popular Democratic United States Senators, two Democratic houses within the state legislature, and four Democratic state constitutional officers. With the state voting for the Democratic candidate in the last three presidential elections, a legitimate argument could be made that the state of Connecticut currently should be considered, in comparison to other states, as politically a more democratic one.[55]

Chapter 2

Connecticut's Constitutions

The Foundation of authority is laid, firstly, in the free consent of the people...
                                                Rev. Thomas Hooker, 1638[1]

Early History

The first state Constitution in Connecticut to be officially labeled as such was created in 1818. But to begin an inquiry about the history of Connecticut's constitution at that date would be to ignore over 150 years of governmental evolution prior to that date that is unique to the state. Long before other states began to wrestle with the structuring of their own political authority, long before the creation of the United States Constitution, Connecticut settled into its own written governmental-structure started by a group of dissatisfied Puritans seeking more land and a better way of life in the New World.

The Reverend Thomas Hooker, originally from England, led a small group of Puritan followers out of the Massachusetts Bay Colony into the Connecticut River Valley in 1636. Adrian Block, a Dutch explorer had started a trading post in this area sometime earlier, but in light of the greater numbers of Englishmen coming into the area, it was abandoned. Hooker established a Congregational Church in what is now the Hartford area. Other settlements were established in Windsor, Wethersfield and Springfield. In one sense, those who settled in Connecticut might have been considered to be something like squatters, having no official royal charter granting them recognition until 1662.[2] The Massachusetts Bay Colony assumed that Connecticut would be under its authority. Other Puritans in England, however, also claimed to have authority over Connecticut, so something called the March Commission, a temporary entity, under the direction of the Massachusetts General Court and composed of two magistrates from each of the four towns of Windsor, Hartford,

Wethersfield and Springfield was set up to be the governing body of this colony until a more permanent settlement could be arranged.[3] A Connecticut General Court was set up in May of 1637 after the March Commission expired. It was composed of three men from each of the four towns, who in turn selected two more men from each town. One man was chosen to be governor. With this development, a self-governing system was begun. By 1638, Springfield left this alliance, leaving the three river towns in Connecticut to establish some rules by which they would attempt to govern themselves.[4]

Hooker, perhaps influenced to a degree by Protestant Reformer John Calvin's idea of locally elected church officials, found a need to voice his concerns about self-government and on May 31, 1638, he delivered what was to become an historic sermon to his followers that outlined his basic thoughts about government and how it should be exercised.[5] Hooker felt that authority should arise from below, not from above.[6] According to Charles Douglas, this sermon focused on three basic principles:

1. The people may appoint their own public officials under God's allowance.

2. The people should exercise this right thoughtfully and seriously according to the will of God.

3. Those public magistrates who have appointed by the people to have power are still limited by the people who gave it to them.[7]

Together, these principles laid the foundation for what some have called the first written framework of government or constitution in the world, the Fundamental Orders.[8] But before such a characterization can be considered, a more detailed discussion of the Fundamental Orders is called for.

The Fundamental Orders

Under Puritan thought, "The first requisite of good government was law." [9] In June of 1638, the General Court appointed a committee to set up rules, articles and agreements for the government of the colony. It is unclear who exactly worked on the document and how it was developed, but Roger Ludlow of Windsor, educated in Oxford and London, was the only trained lawyer at the time in Connecticut. It is generally believed that he played a fundamental role in writing the Fundamental Orders.[10]

The Fundamental Orders contained a preamble and eleven sections or orders.

These sections provided:

1. For a calendar of sessions of the General Court; two each year, the first for elections. A governor and six magistrates are chosen for the General Court.

2. For magistrates to the General Court be voted for democratically.

3. That each of the towns may nominate whomever they wish to serve as deputies.

4. For a Governor who must be a member of an approved congregation; he could not succeed himself as governor.

5. That the second General Court called in the year is for the making of laws.

6. That the Governor sends out warrants for the calling of the two sessions; the freemen of the jurisdiction can petition for a meeting, or meet on their own.

7. For the election of town deputies to the General Court.

8. For additional towns that may join the original three towns and share in this government.

9. For the powers of the deputies of the General Court; the deputies could meet before a session of the General Court for consultation, and they can impose fines.

10. That the General Court has the Supreme power of the Commonwealth. The Governor acts chiefly as moderator and votes in the case of a tie.

11. That taxation was determined by committee of the General Court.[11]

It is significant to note that the Fundamental Orders made no mention of any relationship to the English King. Only certain persons, the "admitted inhabitants" of the towns could actually vote for the deputies or freemen to the General Court. Freemen were adult male landowners who had been declared by town officials as good, upstanding community members. These men usually belonged to the local Puritan church. In turn, the freeman in the colony elected six magistrates who served "at large" and the Governor to the General Court.

Each of the three towns also elected four deputies to the court. Women, children, apprentices, the property-less, indentured servants, Native Africans and indigent Indians were excluded from voting.[12]

The First Constitution?

Were the Fundamental Orders really the first written constitution in the Western world? Over the years there has been considerable debate on this issue. In *History of Connecticut*, published in 1925, Simeon E. Baldwin wrote in no less grand terms, that, "It is the glory of Connecticut that she made for herself the first real Constitution, in the modern sense, known to mankind."[13] William M. Maltbie, a former Chief Justice of the Connecticut Supreme Court wrote this statement which is included in the current *Connecticut State Register and Manual* as a preface to the Fundamental Orders: "In the sense that they were intended to be a framework of government more permanent that the usual orders adopted by the General Court, they were in essence a constitution."[14] On the other side of the argument, as early as the Revolutionary period, State Representative James Davenport of Stamford argued that there was no constitution, but merely laws of the state.[15] Charles M. Andrews asserts that those men that conceived the Fundamental Orders did not view them as organic law that was, "sacrosanct against the General Court's complete control of legislation." Other" fundamental" laws, it should be noted, came into being after the establishment of the original Fundamental Orders by mere order of the General Court.[16] Albert E. Van Dusen asserts that the Fundamental Orders do not appear basic and organic enough to merit the title of "constitution."[17] Perhaps the best commentary on this debate has been articulated by Christopher Collier, Connecticut State Historian. He acknowledges that the Fundamental Orders appear technically, to be no different from simple legislation or a series of statutes passed by a body of representatives.[18] But he also adds that the Fundamental Orders represents a significant occasion where for the first time, people created a government and began to live by it. As such it was a critical initial step to constitutional government in America.[19]

It has been said that the ideas outlined in Thomas Hooker's sermon clearly outlined the concepts of representative and democratic government.[20] While the Fundamental Orders may have outlined some democratic means for electing representatives to the General Court, there was no separation of powers nor checks and balances among branches of government as we might think of in a democratic constitution today. Further, the notion of the people governing themselves was something that was not highly regarded. What might be considered as democracy nowadays, was in the eyes of the Connecticut Puritan seen as an aberration of the human mind and something which did not have divine approval.[21] For the Puritan, democracy, as we might think of it, was very close to anarchy. Election to office was not a way for the people to transmit their authority to an official, but a way for carrying out the will of God.[22] The General Court, as a body, carried out legislative, executive and judicial functions. The governor was required to be a member of an approved church congregation.

The Charter of 1662

By the time that the Fundamental Orders were beginning a new development in government in the Connecticut colony, in England, King Charles I had dissolved Parliament and was ruling by decree. Previously held rights of due process were ignored and forces behind Oliver Cromwell gathered to oppose the King. King Charles I was eventually defeated and a Commonwealth was established with Cromwell as leader in 1653. When Cromwell died in 1658, the struggle for power resumed and the monarchy was restored under Charles II in 1660.[23]

Because the Fundamental Orders had never been officially recognized in England, with the restoration of the king, Connecticut's leaders felt an urgency to send a representative to England to obtain a royal charter which would sustain the lands in the colony and continue the governing system put in place by the Fundamental Orders. Over a period of months, Connecticut's delegation, led by Governor John Winthrop obtained the necessary approvals and the Charter was officially granted on May 10, 1662. It was adopted by the Connecticut General Court as the colony's official law on October 9, 1662.[24]

Under the Charter, the system of government essentially remained the same as under the Fundamental Orders. There were some minor changes. The General Court was now called the General Assembly and the territorial boundaries were expanded to include the New Haven Colony.[25] Essentially, there was a continuation of what had been the situation before.

About this time in England, there was growing sentiment that the New England Colonies would be more economically profitable if they were united under one royal government instead of being separated. They could also more readily be defended against a growing French threat if integrated. In 1686, King James II, a Catholic, gave Major Edmund Andros, an English soldier and aristocrat, a commission as the governor of the new Dominion of New England.[26]

The events which followed this new set of political circumstances established one of Connecticut's most colorful and enduring legends. Andros came to Hartford in October 1687 with troops to demand the old charter. Andros and his party met with the Governor and the Assembly at the meeting house. As the discussion wound on through the day, it grew dark and candles were lit. By some unknown cause, the lights blew out and when they were relit, the charter, which had been brought out to be surrendered, had mysteriously vanished!

· Tradition has it that the Charter had been hidden in the hollow of an oak tree. Subsequently, the "Charter Oak" has become a symbol widely recognized throughout the state of Connecticut and beyond. In 1999, with the minting of a commemorative quarter dollar featuring Connecticut's Charter Oak this symbol of the state has gained national recognition.

Andros did rule the new Dominion of New England from Boston, but only for eighteen months. The Glorious Revolution in England replaced King James II with William and Mary and Parliament reigned supreme, quickly passing a bill of rights and other measures to safeguard and ensure these rights. On May 9, 1689, the General Assembly voted to reinstall the Charter as the basis of Connecticut's government. Not much would change in the structure of state government in Connecticut until 1818 when a Constitution would be adopted.[27]

The Constitution of 1818

In the century following the reestablishment of the Charter in Connecticut, it was felt generally that the established government had served the people of Connecticut well. Politics in the state was characterized as conservative and heavily Federalist.[28] A relatively small group of wealthy men, such as Simeon Baldwin or Daniel Buck, who made their wealth in banking and manufacturing, held great economic and political power within the state.[29] Connecticut was establishing itself as the "land of steady habits" where tradition in government and politics held a very strong position.

Yet, a growing movement for constitutional reform in the state began with the Jeffersonian Republicans and Tolerationists around 1800. Jeffersonian-Republican sentiment characteristically emphasized such concepts as majority rule, the basic natural rights of the individual and a politics based upon consensus.[30]

Especially after the Revolution, it appeared that more and more citizens felt that the government under the Charter in Connecticut was granted by royal decree and never was explicitly approved by the people themselves.[31] In his book, *The Connecticut State Constitution*, Wesley W. Horton argues that three issues in particular emerged which would set the stage for needed Constitutional reform: freedom of religion, separation of powers and the expansion of voting rights.[32]

Freedom of Religion

The Congregational Church had been the established church in Connecticut since the days of Thomas Hooker. Federalist Congregationalists virtually ignored the steady growth of other faiths such as the Baptists and Episcopalians and believed that neither the state nor the Congregational Church could survive without each other. By 1819, there were more non-Congregationalists church societies than Congregationalist ones.[33] According to Horton, attendance at Sunday services was mandatory for Connecticut residents who also had to pay taxes in support of the local Congregational Church. By 1791, if a resident belonged to another church, such as Baptist or Episcopal, a certificate needed to be signed by two civil officers who usually were Congregationalists. A later modification to this law required that dissenters themselves could sign the certificate but that they must be filed with the local established church. These necessities frequently resulted in harassment of non-Congregationalists and prevented other churches from determining where their financial support came from.[34] By 1814, when the War of 1812 came to an end, U.S. Treasury monies designated for the war effort were redistributed back to the states. In Connecticut, most of this money went to Congregationalists with the other religions practiced in the state getting much smaller amounts. This caused an outcry of injustice among the other churches. Ultimately, this proved to be reason for those opposed to the Federalist order to form a coalition among Jeffersonian-Republicans and those in favor of toleration to support a Toleration ticket for governor of the state. Toleration candidate Oliver Wolcott, who had formerly been a Federalist, won the gubernatorial election in 1817. By 1818, consideration of a new constitution reflecting toleration and reform would become a main issue.[35]

Separation of Powers

Coupled with the issue of religious freedom, the issue of government power was becoming more acute. Under the General Assembly there was no separation of powers. In contrast to the Federal government, in Connecticut, the legislature had the supreme power. The governor had no independent power and was elected annually. The members of the judiciary, from the highest state benches to local justices of the peace were appointed annually by the all-powerful state legislature. This system of government promoted few changes in those who would seek and hold office. Once elected, most members of the upper house of the legislature, the Council, and most judicial officers could count on holding their positions until they either voluntarily resigned or died.[36] The magistrates of Connecticut, it might be said, amounted to a "benevolent long term directorate."[37] Noteworthy examples of this kind of development include John Allyn who held the office of secretary of the state for 30 years between 1664 and 1696 and Joseph Whiting, who served as State Treasurer for thirty-nine years from 1679-1718.[38] The emerging Jeffersonian-Republican leaders felt that pursuit of the common good demanded a clearer separation of powers in state government.[39] This matter would become another important issue for the Constitutional Convention.

Expansion of Voting

The right to vote in Connecticut prior to the American Revolution was given primarily to men of at least age twenty-one who owned a minimal amount of real estate. Since at this time many men were able to own such property, many could meet the requirements and vote. As industrialization grew in the state, more and more men did not own property and suffrage laws under Federalist control began to grow stricter to the point where the numbers of those men eligible to vote in the towns across Connecticut were shrinking from their former sizes. It is estimated that by 1816, well under 50 percent of adult white males were eligible to vote.[40] The Federalists in power also enacted a "stand-up" law which literally required voters in the nominating elections to stand up and be counted, instead of casting ballots. This amounted to a blatant attempt to intimidate voters by making their preferences known before wealthy and powerful Federalists who might be moved to take revenge on them at some later time.[41] Thus suffrage expansion and reform became an issue for the Convention of 1818.

The Constitution of 1818 had eleven articles.[42] The first article began with a Declaration of Rights establishing, "essential principles of liberty and free government." Of the twenty-one sections of this article, of particular note was this article's statement on religious worship. Section 3 provided freedom of religious exercise without discrimination to all persons in the state.

Article Second separated the powers of state government into three distinct branches. Article Third was the legislative article. It provided for a Senate composed of twelve members annually elected at large and a House of Representatives chosen annually by the electors of each town. Article Fourth was the executive article and describes the powers and duties of the governor and other executive officers. The Governor now had the ability to veto legislation, but a simple majority of the legislature could override it.[43] Article Fifth was the judicial article and it describes the structure of the judicial system. A Supreme Court of Errors would hear appeals. Article Sixth described the qualifications of electors. It should be noted that one specific qualification was that electors had to be white and male. In Article Seventh, freedom of religion was again explicitly stated in its own article. Article Eighth confirmed the charter of Yale College and supported the public schools throughout the state. Article Ninth described the process of impeachment. Article Tenth prescribed the oath of public office and other general provisions of government. Article Eleventh discussed the amendment process.

Between 1818 and 1965, when the most recent constitutional convention was convened, there were over fifty amendments to the 1818 constitution. The changes addressed all types of issues. For example, the size of the Senate was increased in 1828. The terms of Superior and Supreme court judges were, in 1856, made into eight year terms instead of permanent terms to age seventy. Terms of executive officials were also changed.

Property qualifications for voting were eliminated in 1845, and an amendment requiring the ability to read was added in 1855. In 1876 racial barriers to voting were removed by eliminating the word "white" from the Eighth Amendment and the requirement for being able to read English was added in 1897. There was still representation by Towns in the House of Representatives, despite wide variations in population, making for extremely unfair conditions in the state. Large cities like New Haven could send two delegates to the House while small towns like Union could also send two delegates. New towns with a population of at least 2,500 in 1876 could only have one delegate to send.[44] By 1930, the seven largest cities in the state sent only fourteen of the 267 representatives. These seven cities represented about one-half of the state's population.[45] Another constitutional convention was called to address the representation issue in 1902. It came up with some ideas for reform, but was rejected by the voters.[46]

It was not until 1962 that things in Connecticut began to really change through the federal judicial process. In that year, the U.S. Supreme Court in *Baker v. Carr*[47] ruled that Federal Courts had the duty to review the constitutionality of state legislative apportionment and determine if they violated the equal protection clause of the Fourteenth Amendment. In the apportionment case of *Gray v. Sanders*[48] in 1963, the Court developed the doctrine of "one person, one vote" indicating that representation needed to be as equal as possible within congressional elections. *Westberry v. Sanders*[49] followed in 1964. With the case of *Reynolds v. Simms*,[50] in 1964 the one person, one vote doctrine was extended to the states. In the 1964 case of *Butterworth v. Dempsey*[51] the Federal District Court declared that the mode of representation giving each town equal representation in Connecticut's General Assembly represented an unconstitutional system of apportionment and ordered a reapportionment to assure substantially equal weighting of the votes of all electors.

The 1965 Constitution

At the convening of the Constitutional Convention in 1965, Governor John Dempsey gave the address and stated in simple terms that, "the Federal Court has told us that our form of legislative representation is unconstitutional."[52] The objective was clear: correct the parts of the constitution that denied citizens the right to an equal vote. The convention 1965 resulted in extensive revisions on the previous state constitution. The new constitution, under which the state is currently governed, maintains the tradition of being a concise but broad document of state government. The new Constitution of approximately 7,500 words made it one of the shortest constitutions in the fifty states.[53]

Three new articles were added. After a preamble, **Article First** is essentially a Declaration of Rights. Like the Constitution of 1818, it extensively covers the freedoms of religion, speech, personal liberties, private property and equal protection.

Article Second briefly describes the distribution of powers into legislative, executive and judicial.

Article Third is the legislative article. This article received major revision in that it now ensured that legislative districts for both the house and the senate were consistent with federal constitutional standards in terms of creating electoral districts with equal representation. The national standard of "one person, one vote" was now the standard of representation in Connecticut.

Article Fourth is the executive article. This article describes the state's executive officials. Beyond the governor, there is the lieutenant-governor, secretary of the state, treasurer, comptroller and attorney general. The election and qualifications of each officer are determined in this article.

Article Fifth describes the Judicial Branch. Judicial power in Connecticut is vested in one supreme court, a superior court and lower courts as determined by the General Assembly. This article describes the terms, appointment process and dismissal process of the judges.

Article Sixth determines the qualifications of state electors or those who have the right to vote for state officials. It also allows for the forfeiture of electoral privileges by the conviction of offenses that the General Assembly determines worthy of such forfeiture. Current state statute allows for forfeiture of voting privileges for those convicted of a felony.

Article Seventh states that there is no legal compulsion to join or support any church or religious society. All denominations enjoy equal rights.

Article Eighth states that there shall always be free public elementary and secondary schools in the state. A system of public higher education shall also be maintained in the state.

Article Ninth deals with impeachment of executive and judicial officers. The House of Representatives of the General Assembly has the power to impeach and impeachments are tried in the Senate.

Article Tenth discusses the provision of Home Rule to the towns, cities and boroughs of the state. Prior to 1965, local governments in Connecticut had only those powers granted to them from the state legislature.

Municipal requests for special legislative acts concerning a specific town or city were common and time consuming. In Connecticut, Home Rule efforts began in 1915 with the State Legislature adopting a statute allowing for municipalities to adopt their own governing charters, but this action needed 60 percent of the town's registered voters and soon proved unworkable. In 1951 another similar act was passed with the approval needed down to 51 percent. In 1953 this act was amended with the required approval down to 26 percent of the registered voters of the municipality. Under Home Rule, local governments would have certain powers in areas of local concern.[54] Typical local powers would include certain issues of education, housing, zoning, form of government and property taxation. The article further states that the General Assembly shall enact no special legislation relative to the powers of specific towns except in instances of statewide concern.

Article Eleventh is the general provision article. It prescribes the official oath of office for members of the General Assembly, executive and judicial officers. There is a section under this article for the General Assembly to provide for temporary succession of the powers and duties of all public offices in case of emergency. Another section addresses claims against the state.

Article Twelfth describes the process of proposing and approving amendments to the Constitution. Amendments may be proposed by members of either the Senate or the House. If they receive at least a majority of the members of each house, the amendment is continued to the regular session of the General Assembly elected at the next general election. If the amendment, having been continued as stated, is again approved by a majority of the total membership of each house, the Secretary of the State transmits the amendment to the town clerk in each town, where it will be voted upon at the next general election. It a majority of electors approve the amendment, it becomes a part of the constitution.

The Thirteenth and last article addresses methods of convening constitutional conventions. Two-thirds of the total membership of each house of the General Assembly can call for a convention not earlier than ten years from the last convention. Or, at the even numbered year general election following the twenty years from the last convention, the question, "Shall there be a Constitutional Convention to amend or revise the Constitution of the state?" shall be submitted to the electors of the state. If a majority vote yes, the general assembly shall provide for such a convention. This question was put to the electors in 1986 which was the even numbered election year following twenty years after the convention of 1965. A majority of the electors of Connecticut answered no. It further provides for another twenty year period from the date of when the amendment question was last asked.

Article Fourteenth provides for the approval of the constitution by the people of the state and the proclamation of the governor.

Since its adoption in 1965, Connecticut's constitution has been amended twenty-nine times. Some of these amendments include: lowering the voting age to eighteen; removal of the waiting period to be eligible to vote; expansion of equal protection to the mentally and physically disabled; establishing an appellate court; establishing a mandatory retirement age for judges at age seventy and most recently, establishing rights for victims of crime.

A Recent Constitutional Issue

In Connecticut, traditionally, the wealthier towns, with higher property taxes, could afford to spend more for public services, especially education. In 1977, in a case called *Horton v. Meskill*,[55] Connecticut's Supreme Court affirmed a lower court's decision that essentially found that relying on the widely variable local property tax to finance public education violated a student's guarantee to equal rights and equal protection.

In response to this ruling, the Connecticut legislature created the Minimum Expenditure Requirement (MER) that towns would have to spend on education and the Guaranteed Tax Base (GTB), a formula grant program for helping school districts in need to meet the MER. Another formula grant program called Education Cost Sharing (ECS) replaced the GTB for the same purpose and currently remains in place as the mechanism for state funding for local public education.[56] Some have argued that these state efforts have not yet achieved the desired results. "The ECS formula has become so complicated and so politically driven that it has not accomplished what the legislature intended, despite being tinkered with every year since it was approved."[57]

Beginning in 1989, another suit was filed in state court in behalf of school students in the Hartford area against then Governor of Connecticut William O'Neil, the State Board of Education and other education officials. Widely known as the *Sheff v. O'Neil*[58] case, the suit charged that with the high concentration of poor, racially segregated students in city schools, the school children were deprived of their constitutional rights to equal educational opportunity. The plaintiffs alleged that State statutes that required that school district lines conform with municipal boundary lines created "de facto" segregation. After making its way through the state judicial system, in 1996 the Supreme Court found that Article Eight, which guarantees the right to an education, is informed by Article First, which prohibits racial discrimination and segregation. Taken together, the Constitution therefore, prohibits the type of extreme segregation that is in existence in Hartford's public school system.[59] The Supreme Court found that the State was obligated to address this inequity. The state's response since the decision has generally been to work to improve the quality and outcomes of public education statewide. The General Assembly responded with P.A. 97-290, legislation which is aimed at reducing throughout the state racial, ethnic and economic isolation. Included under this law is the development of charter and magnet schools, sister schools, inter-district programs and projects, distance learning and other experiences that increase awareness of diversity and cultures. Since the Sheff decision, there were questions on how the state will implement the decision and address the racial and economic segregation issue in Connecticut. The Sheff plaintiffs went back to court to argue that P.A. 97-290 had not adequately addressed the inequities brought out in the original Sheff case.

The Superior Court ruled against them in 1999 stating that more time was needed to see if the methods outlined in the law would indeed improve the equality of education in Connecticut.[60] A settlement was finally reached in 2003.

Equity in education continues to be an unresolved issue in Connecticut. In 1998, in a Superior court case referred to as *Johnson v. Rowland*, a group of students from various towns in the state have argued that the current formula (ECS) for granting state aid to education has still denied them an equal educational opportunity.[61]

Chapter 3

CONNECTICUT POLITICAL PARTIES AND ELECTIONS

Parties, to some extent, will exist in all free governments, but in this country, the constitution, the fundamental form of government, is adapted to call them into existence and perpetuate them.

Noah Webster, 1843[1]

American political parties in general are private associations permitted to conduct their activities and business in private and that business mainly is primarily to identify candidates for public office and win elections. Noah Webster was no great supporter of political parties, considering them a cause of frustration for unity and corruption for public officials. However, these private associations are strictly regulated by state laws. State laws generally may define how a party becomes eligible for a place on an election ballot, the requirements for party membership, and regulate the selection of officers, meetings and campaign spending.

Sarah McCally Moorehouse has said, "The nature of each state government depends upon the leaders who run it. And that leadership is determined, for better or worse, by the political party system."[2] Traditionally, political parties at the state level have assumed several roles in the political process. They provide organizational continuity, endorsements of candidates, grassroots support for local efforts, financial and technical support for candidates, legislative support and links to the national parties and candidates. Specifically, parties help candidates by contributing money to their campaigns, distributing campaign literature, organizing phone banks, distributing lawn signs, door to door canvassing and conducting opinion polls.[3]

Party History in Connecticut

According to Norman Stamps, political parties were slow to

develop in Connecticut. One of the reasons for this was that from early on there were only two principal industries in the state; farming and commerce. Many of the people living in early Connecticut were narrow in outlook and were more concerned with local matters rather than issues of statewide or nationwide importance. Thus, there were few issues around which political parties could form at the grassroots level and capture the interest of the people.[4]

In its early history, several parties emerged within the state. The Federalists, The Toleration Party, the Abolition Party, the Whig Party, the Liberty Party, and the Know-Nothing Party, all arose around a particular issue or set of issues, merged, were modified and changed or faded away.

From the Civil War to the New Deal, Connecticut was traditionally under control of the Republican Party. Connecticut's original system of representation, before reapportionment, when small towns had as much electoral power as densely populated cities, helped to assure this control. Nearly 90 percent of these small towns were Republican and sent their Republican representatives to the House of Representatives in the General Assembly.[5]

Three factors helped to develop Connecticut's Republican character. A sense of Conservative traditionalism among the people, the growing support for the Republican Party by the state's manufacturers and the popular distrust of the Democrats due to the experience of the Civil War.[6] During its Revolutionary history, Connecticut leaders emerged who favored a strong national government and strong economy and were able to prevail over small farmers who believed that national political centralization would be harmful. Connecticut's leaders realized that a strong national government could preserve the conservative respect for authority that they had established in the Land of Steady Habits and promote a strong economy. The most useful natural resource was the resourcefulness of the inventors and manufacturers. When railroads and canals brought grains to the east cheaply, Connecticut farmers could not compete. They either went West to the frontier or to the cities to work as laborers.[7] The National Republican Party stood for protectionism for American industry and high tariffs so it was natural that workers at this time supported the Republican Party.[8] The Union, led by Republican President Lincoln was victorious in the Civil War, and Connecticut, which had already abolished slavery in the state in 1848, shared the outlook of other northern states in their general support of Lincoln in preserving the Union. In the aftermath of the war, many returning veterans argued that to vote for

Democrats would be heretical.[9] In the 73-year period from 1858 to 1931, Republicans held the governor's office for almost 57 years.[10]

In the 1920s, J. Henry Roraback, of small town and conservative background, emerged as a powerful leader of the Republican State Central Committee. He was able to combine money from business, rural organization and a conservative governmental policy into a tight political machine.[11] In this era, Republicans controlled both the executive and legislative branches in Connecticut government. For Roraback, competence in business implied competence to render public service in the state.[12] As president of several utility companies and serving as a director for insurance companies and a bank, Roraback held a strong belief that in helping the business interests of Connecticut, he was serving the interests of the state.[13] Suffering from ill health, he committed suicide in 1937.[14]

In 1940, Connecticut Republicans demonstrated their strength and resourcefulness at the national stage. The sixteen Connecticut delegates to the Republican national convention in Pittsburgh that year cast votes for Wilkie on every ballot and Wilkie won the nomination. Connecticut governor Raymond Baldwin gave the seconding speech for Wilkie telling the convention that Wilkie had, "the pioneering spirit that is typical of Connecticut." Wilkie lost the election, but some would claim that his campaign helped to mold American support of taking a more active role in international affairs and Connecticut Republicans played a key role in that development.[15]

The Democratic Party took longer to gather strength. Support for this party traditionally came from the cities and urban centers. It was the party of the immigrants, Catholics and the poor.[16] Several factors were responsible for the development of the Democratic Party in the state. These included the immigration of groups of people into Connecticut that supported the Democratic Party, the Al Smith presidential campaign and the Wall Street Crash. Beginning in the 1880s, large numbers of immigrants from both western and eastern Europe carrying with them their religious traditions began to settle in Connecticut's urban areas. The Catholic Italians and Irish were the largest and most political of these new immigrants. Since the presidency of Andrew Jackson, who welcomed the support of Catholics, this religious group tended to be democratic.[17] Because these groups formed the core of manual labor available in the cities, unions, also supportive of the Democratic Party, were an important influence on them. The presidential campaign of Catholic candidate Al Smith in 1928 won strong support from Democrats and served to solidify the strength of the party. By the end of the 1920s Connecticut had become a very industrialized state, employing great numbers of workers at good wages. When the stock market crashed and the Depression ensued, thousands of people lost their jobs, homes and farms. The Republican supported business community began to loose the trust of the people who also felt that the Republican backed government of the state was not doing enough to assist them through these hard times. The result was that Wilbur Cross, a Democrat and former dean at Yale, became governor in 1930. The election of the very popular Franklin D. Roosevelt in 1932 worked to solidify the presence of Democratic power in Connecticut.[18]

John Bailey, a graduate of Harvard Law School, became chairman of the State Democratic Party in 1946 and soon became a powerful force who was able to create winning coalitions of ethnic groups and working class people who supported the Democratic Party. He was not very successful in his own political campaigns. He lost an effort for Democratic precinct captain early in his career and later failed in a general election for Hartford County Probate Judge. Yet this political boss's sharp ability to organize and influence party supporters on a full-time basis around Democratic issues helped the party secure its place as a contender in Connecticut politics and earned Bailey the characterization as, "the perfect Machiavelli."[19] For his efforts as liaison with state and local political leaders throughout the country in the 1960 presidential campaign, President Kennedy appointed him to the Chairmanship of the Democratic National Committee, a post he served concurrently as state party chairman. It also probably didn't hurt that both men were Harvard educated and Irish Catholic. The successful campaigns of Governors Abraham Ribicoff, John Dempsey and Ella Grasso were also orchestrated by Bailey's relentless behind-the-scenes political talents.

Bailey's keen interest and ability in politics left its mark upon his children. It is notable that Bailey's daughter, Barbara Kennelly, was a very successful United States Congresswoman for Connecticut until she was defeated in the 1996 race for governor by John Rowland. His son, John M. Bailey had been Connecticut's Chief State's Attorney beginning in 1993 but stepped down from the post in late 2002 for health reasons.

In his study of Connecticut State Senators, Grant Reeher discussed how Republicans have been characterized as being concerned about fiscal responsibility, budget deficits and tax increases. Democrats have seemed to work hard in providing needed services and seem to be more focused on people.[20] In the 2002 session, the 36-member State Senate had twenty-one Democrats and fifteen Republicans. The House of Representatives is considerably Democratic having about two-thirds of its total of 151 members within that party. Democratic House Speaker Moira Lyons attributed her party's success in the 2000 state house elections to back-to-basic campaigning, which included finding talented people who were willing to work hard.[21] From the perspective of the capitol city, the strength of the Democratic party, claims Robert Jackson, chair of the Hartford Democratic Town Committee in 1999, comes from, "the fact that it is the party of the people-respecting individual differences, and celebrating diversity, tolerance and fellowship."[22]

Since 1930, competition between both parties in Connecticut, for the most part, has been the norm. This is supported by an index developed by Austin Ranney which measures party competition and control in the states. By looking at such factors as the percentage of votes won by the parties in gubernatorial elections and the percentage of seats won by the parties in each house of the legislature, the length of time the parties controlled the governorship and legislature, and the proportion of time the governorship and the legislature has been divided between the two parties, he derived a measure of government control by party. On his index, a score of zero meant complete Republican control; a score of one meant complete Democratic control. A score of .500 meant a highly competitive party environment where control is evenly split. Ranney examined competition in Connecticut between 1956-1970 and calculated a score of .5732, indicating a healthy state of two-party competition.[23] Bibby, Cotter, Gibson and Huckshorn, using Ranney's index, looked at party control from 1981-1988 and came up with an index score of .58 showing Connecticut still being a competitive two-party state.[24] The index was updated for 1995-1999 by Bibby and Holbrook. The most recent score for Connecticut is .486, a very competitive party environment where party control over government is fairly split.[25] Over time it seems that Connecticut, while at times capable of tilting towards one party appears fairly evenly competitive. This is well illustrated by an examination of our state's gubernatorial elections results since 1925 which reveals that there have been eight Democratic governors, eight Republican governors and one third-party governor.

Over the last several decades the breakout of political party affiliation is revealed in the following table:

Table 3.1 Party Affiliation in Connecticut

	1966	1976	1986	1996	1998
Democrats	458,730	625,419	670,468	668,247	699,766
Republicans	381,000	428,214	445,745	470,774	477,684
Other	0	754	941	3,511	4,561
Unaffiliated	484,359	614,973	555,795	727,381	787,313
Total	**1,324,092**	**1,669,360**	**1,672,949**	**1,869,913**	**1,969,324**

Source: *Secretary of the State, Connecticut State Register and Manual*,
       various years.

This chart shows that voter registration continues to increase and that the Democratic Party continues to register more voters than the Republican. It is also clear that in the last decade, the unaffiliated voters have the greatest numbers and thus have held the balance of which party wins an election.

Parties in Decline?

It has been argued by McKee and Peterson that the presidential election of 1976 signaled the decline in party power in Connecticut. In that year, which saw the first presidential primary in Connecticut, the National Democratic Party imposed new rules for the state party to conform with. The result of these rules, which required the party to be more open and adhere to affirmative action requirements, was the weakening of party discipline in terms of procedures and patronage.[26] Gary Rose adds that with this decline, the quality of politics in the state has suffered, exhibiting a "lack of linkage between the people and the political process."[27]

Another reason cited for the decline of party power in Connecticut was the removal of the party lever from voting machines. By a popular vote, a statewide constitutional amendment removing the party levers was approved by voters in 1986.[28] In terms of legislative campaigns at the state level, it has been argued that legislators do not rely much anymore on the party organizations for their campaigns. The services that the party traditionally provided, have been overshadowed by a candidate's own personal organization.[29]

A review of the gubernatorial races in 1986 and 1990 show another reason for party decline: internal infighting within both parties during the nomination process. In 1986, the Republicans experienced a three way primary race between Richard Bozzuto, Gerald Labriola and Julie Belaga, in which Belaga eventually became the party's nominee. John Rowland in 1990 emerged as the Republican's candidate in a clear convention victory but the Democrats displayed the same kind of infighting between Governor William O'Neil and Congressman Bruce Morrison. While Morrison received the convention's nomination, William Cibes, an O'Neil supporter, received 20 percent of the convention's delegates allowing him to force a statewide primary.[30] The end result of the 1990 governor's race saw Lowell P. Weicker Jr., a former Republican U.S Senator, winning the election as an independent candidate, the only such winner of the 20th century. Some who study the state's political parties, like Gary Rose, fear that parties in the state may have already headed down the road marked by decline and deterioration.[31] Despite these negative developments regarding the parties, McKee and Peterson offer a positive note: the state parties continue to play a role in organizing citizens and in general the political environment remains competitive.[32]

The Mechanics of Party Membership In Connecticut

According to Connecticut General Statute 9-372, a major party in Connecticut is defined by; a) a party whose candidate for Governor received at least 20 percent of the total vote for that office at the last gubernatorial election or b) a party whose enrolled membership, as of the last gubernatorial election, is at least 20 percent of the total enrollment of all political parties in the state. In Connecticut, both the Republican and Democratic parties currently have major party status. In the 1990 state election, when Lowell Weicker ran successfully for governor as a third party candidate in a three-way race, the Democratic candidate, Bruce Morrison, barely managed to receive just over the 20 percent of the total vote.

Article IX of the Connecticut Constitution gives qualified residents of Connecticut's towns who are eighteen years old the right to vote. According to Connecticut General Statutes 9-45 and 9-45a, citizens of Connecticut who have committed a disenfranchising felony and have been punished by confinement in a correctional facility are erased from their voting district lists and lose their right to vote. Voting rights may be restored once written proof is provided to the registrar of voters that demonstrates all fines associated with the conviction have been paid, that discharge from confinement has occurred and if applicable, there has been discharge from parole.

If you are a new voter in the state and join a party upon registration, you immediately have the privilege of voting in a party primary or caucus. If you are already registered as an unaffiliated voter, and want to enroll in a party, you make a written application to your local town's Registrar of Voters. Both new and unaffiliated voters must enroll by noon the day before a primary or caucus in order to vote in that primary or caucus. If you are changing from one party to another, you must make written application to the local registrars, but you have to wait three months before participating in a caucus or primary of your new party. In Connecticut, party conventions generally nominate candidates for office. The local town committee or caucus of each party endorses candidates for local office and delegates for state and district conventions. While these endorsements can be overturned by a primary challenge this wasn't always the case in Connecticut. In 1955, with Public Act 51, Connecticut became the last state in the United States to finally allow defeated candidates at a convention to challenge the endorsed candidate with a primary.[33]

Elections

As a fundamental process within democratic society, it is through victorious elections that candidates attain political office. There are general elections, in which the victor assumes the office and primary elections, where the victor within a party earns the right to represent the party in the general election.

A primary is an election held within a party, prior to the general election, to challenge a candidate endorsed by the party organization. Primaries are held when a nomination or position is contested. If the election is local, according to Connecticut General Statute 9-406, the right to primary is obtained by filing a petition with the town clerk containing the signatures of 5 percent of the enrolled party members eligible to vote for that office. For statewide office under the challenge primary law introduced in 1955, the challenger must have received at least 15 percent of the delegate vote at the party convention to file for a primary against the convention winner. Minor party nominations are not subject to primary in accordance with Connecticut General Statute 9-400(b). In March of 2002, the Brennan Center for Justice at New York University School of Law filed a suit on

behalf of several plaintiffs in United States District Court against the constitutionality of this law, claiming that it violated the First Amendment
rights of other candidates seeking to challenge the endorsed candidates.
In hearing this case, which has come to be referred to as *Campbell v.
Bysiewicz,* in August 2002, a U.S District Court judge questioned the
constitutionality of this law and ruled that any registered party member
could seek to be on the party's primary ballot. A federal Court of Appeals
overruled the decision, but political parties portend inevitable change in
this process in the near future.[34]

By a decision of the United States Supreme Court, *Tashjian v.
Connecticut,*[35] voters who are registered as unaffiliated may be allowed
to vote in a party primary if the state party committee permits these voters as well as those registered with the party to do so. Connecticut has a
closed primary system. Voters here must be registered in a party to vote
in a partisan election and they can only vote in the party in which they are
registered.

Both major parties in Connecticut are run by state central committees headed by a chairperson. State committees are composed of members elected by county committees, state and congressional district conventions or party primaries. Both state central committees perform a variety of tasks. They call state conventions to nominate candidates, adopt
party policies, raise funds, assist with campaigns, assist local party units
and perform public relations. The state chairpersons act as head of the
party organization and of fund-raising efforts, recruit candidates, generate party publicity and serve as a liaison with national and local party
organizations.

Chris DePino, chairman of the Republican State Central Committee has stressed that the Republican Party's main mission in Connecticut is to do one thing: elect Republicans. It does this from a service point
of view. For Depino, two concepts are equally important. Conducting the
business of politics, that is, managing the media, finding and supporting
candidates, raising money and filing reports goes hand-in-hand with conducting politics as a business. This means running the organization as
efficiently as possible under a business plan, using available technology
to its fullest extent and staffing party headquarters with competent and
professional people.[36] John F. Droney, Jr., State Democratic Chairman in
1988 said in an interview with Gary Rose, that as chair, he served as, "the
advisor, confidante, tactician, ombudsman, fundraiser, dispenser of patronage, media spokesperson and lighting rod for candidates."[37]

Running for Office

Joseph Lieberman has been a Connecticut state senator, Connecticut state Attorney General and is currently a United States Senator from Connecticut seeking the presidency. As someone who has spent most of his life in public service, the example he offers is noteworthy for prospective candidates at any level, no matter what their political ideology or party affiliation. Lieberman says that if you are going to run for political office, you need to really enjoy people.[38] In his book, *In Praise of Public Life*, he offers several points to consider for anyone who would run for elective office. Among them are included:

1. Raising money for the campaign is critical.

2. The need to utilize electronic media: television, radio and the internet.

3. Going door to door to meet the people is still important.

4. It is helpful to realize that sometimes success in politics requires luck, beyond all the hard work.[39]

At a more local level, Jason Jakubowski is a serious young man full of energy and a real interest in politics. In 1999 he ran for one of fifteen seats on the Board of Aldermen in New Britain, a city of about 71,500, and won his first elective office as the second highest vote getter on the board. Two years later, he was elected to his second term. He identifies five key factors for his electoral success: Party affiliation, Name recognition, Ethnicity, Crossover appeal and Campaigning. Jakubowski is a Democrat running in a historically Democratic, urban community. His campaign emphasized getting his name out, taking advantage of whatever opportunities arose. It helped that New Britain is heavily populated by people of Polish decent and the ethnicity of the name Jakubowski resonated with many voters. While generally loyal to his party, his sense of independence helped him pull in crossover votes. Finally, in his estimate, Jakubowski covered at least 30 percent of the city of New Britain campaigning door-to-door. Meeting people face-to-face still makes an impression at the polls.[40]

Uncontested Elections

Family obligations, two-career families, and just the lack of time all take their toll on those who would run for elective office. At the local level, it seems that it is becoming, in some areas of Connecticut, harder to find candidates for local boards and commissions.[41] McKee and Peterson report that there has been a general rise in uncontested elections in Connecticut since 1980. In 1996, there were forty-one total uncontested state elections in Connecticut. In House of Representative elections, the Republicans did not contest twenty-four races; the Democrats did not contest seventeen.[42] In the 1998 state elections for the General Assembly, there were forty-one uncontested races for both the House and Senate.[43] In the November 2000 state assembly elections, seventy-one of 187 state legislators had "no opponent willing to take the time, or raise the money to run."[44]

Campaign Finance

Since 1990, thirty states have made radical changes in their campaign finance laws. For example, Hawaii and Ohio give tax credits to contributors. Ohio and North Dakota prevent labor unions from contributing to candidate campaigns. Arkansas and California, like Connecticut, have placed limits on how much an individual can give to a party or political action committee (PAC).[45] The cost of running political campaigns in the states are ever increasing. Candidates for Governor in Connecticut spent $10.2 million in 1994. In one state senatorial race in 1996, the two candidates raised more that $300,000. From 1986-1996, the costs of races for state representative had risen by 64 percent.[46] Finding ways to finance a political campaign have become critical to a candidate's political success, but regulating the process fairly has also become critical and difficult. Beginning in 1987 to 2000 a total of twenty-six bills regarding campaign financing in Connecticut have been raised in the General Assembly.

In 1999, House Bill 7019 establishing voluntary public financing of campaigns was defeated. According to State Senator Louis D. DeLuca from Redding, "Our state has already enacted some of the strictest campaign finance laws in the nation."[47]

The Republican and Democratic National Parties received $463.1 million in soft money in the 1999-2000 election cycle. The American Federation of State, County and Municipal Employees (AFSCME) contributed $10.3 million and the Community Workers of America gave $6 million to the Democrats. The Republicans received $7.4 million from Philip Morris Companies and $3.7 from the American Financial Group.[48]

In many states, soft money from the national parties can be passed on to their state counter parts. Federal law distinguishes between federal accounts of national party committees and other non-federal accounts that they may have. The federal accounts are the ones used directly for federal elections, subject to federal disclosure and contribution limitations. Soft money contributions, on the other hand, are the kind that come under the heading of non-federal and are thus freer from public and federal scrutiny. In theory, this type of money is to be used for "party building" activities such as getting out the vote drives. It can be used to help party candidates at the state levels. The Democratic National Party, for example, in 1996 transferred almost $1 million to the Connecticut State Democratic Party.[49] In 1999, Public Act 98-7 came into effect in Connecticut which banned these kinds of soft money transfers into the state's political parties.

Connecticut election and campaign financing laws found in Chapter 150 of the *Connecticut General Statutes* have explicit provisions which impose specific limits on the amount of money business and labor PACs may contribute to political campaigns .

For example, contributions of up to $2,500 may be made to a candidate for governor from an individual or from a political committee. A political committee established by a business entity may contribute up to $5,000 for a candidate for governor. There are no limits to contributions made from a state central or town party committee to a candidate for governor. Other state offices have lesser contribution limits. For example, committees may contribute to candidates for Secretary of the State and Treasurer up to $1,500; contributions to State Representatives may be up to $250 from individuals or political committees or up to $500 if they are from political committees established by business entities. However, the law is essentially silent on amounts of money given by "ideological" type PACs. Section 9-333t of this chapter of the statutes states that "a political committee organized for ongoing political activities, may make unlimited contributions," to party and candidate committees.

The Recent Rise in Minor Party Candidates

Third party emergence is generally associated with the quality of performance and the public's perception of the major parties. With the recent popularity of Ross Perot and Ralph Nader at the national level and the successes of Jessie Ventura and Lowell Weicker at the state level, there has been a noticeable increase in the rise of minor party candidates beginning in the 1990s. Says Governor Ventura about the power of third parties, "Third parties can still drive the agenda. We can because the [major parties] want to stop us."[50] This development points to the important role that third parties have in raising issues, mobilizing new voters, and shifting the balance from one candidate to another in close races.[51]

In November 1990, Lowell P. Weicker Jr., former U.S. Senator, became the first independent to be elected to governor of Connecticut in the 20th century winning as the candidate from the newly formed A Connecticut Party. His opponents questioned his ability to govern if he was elected without major party support. Weicker ran on a platform that aimed to clean up state government, claiming that surplus revenues had been squandered and that bureaucracy had become too large. He won with just over 40 percent of the votes and soon promoted and secured the passage of a state income tax.[52]

A minor party comes into existence through a nominating petition which any registered Connecticut voter can apply for. This is a formal written application requesting a certain number of Connecticut registered voters to place names on the state's election ballot by signing such application. Minor parties in Connecticut are defined by Connecticut General Statute 9-372. A minor party is a party whose candidate for a particular office received at the last election, at least 1 percent of the whole number of votes cast for all the candidates for that office.

Minor parties eligible to nominate candidates in Connecticut for the November 2000 election, and their active enrollments included the following:[53]

Concerned Citizens	127
Green	1,024
Libertarian	653
Reform	505
Independence	372
Independent	666
Pro-Bethel	3
B.A.C.	2
Independent Party of Norwalk	764
A Portland Party	1
Southington Independent	5
Save Westport Now	0
A Sentinel Party	42

In Connecticut, there appears to be an acceptance of the validity of third parties due to a decline in traditional party loyalties, a general distrust of the status quo and an openness for new approaches to solving problems. In July 13-21, 1999 a survey done by the Center for Survey Research and Analysis at the University of Connecticut and *The Hartford Courant* found that 68 percent of those asked felt it was a good idea to have third party candidates in the presidential elections.[54] It should be noted that Lowell Weicker's party, A Connecticut Party, does not appear on the above list of minor party enrollments. It faded away shortly after Governor Weicker's term ended.

Chapter 4

The Connecticut General Assembly
and Connecticut Lobbies

The legislative process is like a river that is being fed by many streams. Some are bigger than others but they all enter and become part of the flow. So too with the legislative process. Many individuals and groups influence the process but no one always dominates.

Joseph Lieberman
Former Connecticut State Senator
and Current U.S. Senator[1]

The idea of elected, representative government in the state has its origins in the Fundamental Orders. Yet the General Assembly today bears little resemblance to the body that created laws over 350 years ago. The legislative body for the State of Connecticut is called the General Assembly. It is a bicameral legislature, with a lower house composed of representatives and an upper house composed of senators. Because the legislature in Connecticut is not a full-time one, it is sometimes considered to be a citizen-legislature. Members often have other careers or livelihoods that they must balance with their public service responsibilities. Rank and file members earn a basic salary of $28,000 with additional compensation for holding leadership positions. The main purpose of the General Assembly, as for every other representative state government, is to enact laws for the state. The chief responsibilities of individual legislators is threefold: representing constituents, law-making and legislative oversight .[2]

Origins of the General Assembly

The legislature in Connecticut, as outlined in the Fundamental Orders, began under the name of the General Court. This was a unicameral body consisting of six magistrates, and one governor chosen by the freemen of the colony. In addition, the three towns of Windsor, Wethersfield and Hartford, sent four deputies each. This unicameral structure recognized no separation of powers, exercising all executive, legislative and judicial powers.[3]

With the Charter of 1662, the General Court became known as the General Assembly, the name it still retains. An early principle of Connecticut government under the Fundamental Orders was equal representation in the General Assembly by town, not by the size of the town's population.[4] By the 1700s, each town was electing two representatives to send to the General Assembly. In 1780, as the General Assembly began to become crowded, newly incorporated towns were given only one vote instead of two.[5] By 1874, a Constitutional change allowed towns which had reached a population of 5,000 to have two votes in the General Assembly. Those with smaller populations had one representative, but the towns which had previously enjoyed two representatives prior to this, regardless of their population, were allowed to keep them.[6]

The 1818 Constitution provided that there would be twelve Senators to be elected at large. In 1828, a constitutional amendment specified that the state would be divided into eighteen to twenty-four senatorial districts, which would ensure "a proper equality between the districts."[7] A constitutional convention was called in 1902 to address issues of disparate representation, but Connecticut's voters rejected the minimal reforms that had been agreed to in convention. The Senate was finally redistricted in 1903, but the House remained severely mal-apportioned. For example, in 1900, both Union, population 428 and Hartford, population 108,000 each had two representatives to the General Assembly.[8] As previously discussed in Chapter Two, it took several decisions of the United States Supreme Court, ie., *Baker v. Carr, Wesberry v. Sanders*, and *Reynolds v. Simms*, to address these types of problems that were occurring across the states and establish the concept that one person's vote should be equal to another's. Washington Columnist David Broder, in discussing recent strides made by state legislatures, has said that these early court decisions ended the control of state legislatures by, "rural court house gangs." In the decades since, state legislatures have expanded their staffs and research capabilities and have begun to develop their own expertise that have helped free them from the dominance of the governors and executive agencies.[9] These decisions forced the General Assembly to call for a convention in 1965 to seriously address the reapportionment issue.

The Convention, held in the summer of 1965, agreed on a House of Representatives which would seat between 125 and 225 members and a Senate which would seat between thirty and fifty members. Also, the General Assembly would be responsible for redistricting itself following each federal census. Under the new redistricting plan drawn by the General Assembly, each representative and senator, within their respective districts, would be representing approximately the same number of people.[10]

Membership and Organization

Article Two of the Amendments to the Connecticut Constitution requires that members of the Connecticut General Assembly must be twenty-one years old and reside in the district which they represent. They are elected in November of even-numbered years. There are presently 151 assembly districts and thirty-six Senate districts with one representative or senator from each district. All serve a two-year term. The General Assembly meets in long sessions and short sessions. The long sessions convene in odd-numbered years on the Wednesday following the first Monday in January and adjourns not later than the Wednesday following the first Monday in June. The short sessions convene in even-numbered years on the Wednesday following the first Monday in February and adjourns not later than Wednesday following the first Monday in May. In the short sessions, the General Assembly can only work on budgetary, financial or revenue items, bills and resolutions raised by committee and those matters certified by both the Speaker and President Pro Temp to be emergencies. This is noted in Article Third of the Amendments to the Constitution. Special sessions of the General Assembly may be called by either the General Assembly itself or by the governor. If the governor vetoes a bill at the end of the regular session, the General Assembly must be convened in a special post adjournment session to reconsider the vetoed bill.

Under Article Third, Section 13 of the Connecticut Constitution, both the House and the Senate adopt their own sets of rules at the beginning of each session. The House elects a Speaker to preside over its business along with a majority leader elected by the members of the majority party and a minority leader, elected by the minority parties members. There are also a host of "deputy" and "assistant" leaders and whips for both majority and minority parties. The lieutenant governor presides over the Senate as President. The Senate elects a President Pro Tempore to preside in the absence of the President. Majority and Minority leaders are elected by their respective parties. The President Pro Tempore of the Senate and the Speaker of the House appoint rank and file members to their committee assignments. There are also clerks who maintain the records of the proceedings and assistant clerks, messengers and door-keepers that assist in the distribution of documents. These are appointed by the leadership of their respective chambers.[11]

Much of the work of any legislative body gets accomplished within committees. Committees hold hearings to learn more about the issues that come to them, members offer amendments to bills that are being considered, compromises on some bills are negotiated through de-bate and life and death decisions of other bills are made. Unlike many other state legislatures, the committees of the General Assembly are joint committees, being composed of members of both the House and the Sen-ate and serving throughout the year. Senators typically serve on four or five committees, Representatives serve on three or four committees. There were twenty-two standing committees and four select committees during the 2001-2002 term. These were committees on:

- Aging
- Appropriations
- Banks
- Children
- Commerce
- Education
- Energy and Technology
- Environment
- Executive and Legislative Nominations
- Finance, Revenue and Bonding
- General Law
- Government Administration and Elections
- Housing
- Human Services
- Insurance and Real Estate
- Internship
- Judiciary
- Labor and Public Employees
- Legislative Management
- Planning and Development

- Program Review and Investigations
- Public Health
- Public Safety
- Regulation and Review
- Transportation

Each of these committees has a House chair and a Senate chair composed of members of the majority party who share duties and responsibilities. The chairs tend to be very influential within their respective committees.[12]

Legislative Behavior

In his study of the Connecticut Senate, *Narratives of Justice*, in which he probed Connecticut state senators on their thoughts about distributive justice, Grant Reeher also outlined several factors, from both an internal and external perspective, that have seemed to influence the behavior of the upper house of the General Assembly. Important internal factors for Reeher are: limitations or constraints of time, the committee and chair system, party leadership, professionalization and the legislative support staff. These factors acknowledge that Connecticut's legislature is technically part-time and comprised of citizen-legislators, that committees are interdependent for expertise, that political parties still retain a degree of control as legislative organizers, and that the legislature continues to improve its performance through the employment of professional and technical expertise to assist it in carrying out its duties.[13] This last factor is illustrated with the developments in supporting offices that came with legislative reforms after the 1965 Constitutional Convention. After the new constitution came legislation in 1969 that created the Joint Committee on Legislative Management, which in turn created the Office of Legislative Research, which provides information to members about nonfiscal matters, and the Office of Fiscal Analysis, which provides information on financial matters.[14] The Legislative Commissioners Office is a bipartisan commission directed by attorneys from each party providing legal expertise and services in bill drafting and development.[15]

Important external factors for Reeher include: other actors such as the governor, lobbyists and the media, the needs of constituents, the state of the economy, public opinion and interstate competition. Factors like these remind us no legislative body acts in isolation and that there are influences near and far beyond the legislative chambers which require attention if legislators are to be effective in their roles.[16]

The Process of Making Laws in Connecticut

Every year at the state capitol there may be thousands of bills that are proposed. Only a relative few eventually become law. Future laws begin their life as "proposed" bills written in plain language, which are filed by members of either house with the Clerk of that house. The clerk issues a title and number and lists the sponsors which are printed in the House and Senate journals. Sponsors can be either a legislator or a committee. Senate bills are identified as S.B. and have a number ranging from 1-4,999. House bills are identified as H.B and have a number equal to or greater than 5,000. It is therefore possible to identify a bill as originating in either the House or the Senate by its number. The bill is then sent to the appropriate committee depending on the subject matter. Committees may have the bill drafted in legal language, combine it with other bills and have it drafted as a "committee bill," send the bill to another committee, take no action, or take the bill and rewrite it in statutory form as a new "raised" committee bill. The committees then hold public hearings on the bill. Different outcomes may result. The committees may report out the bill favorably, giving it a "Favorable Report," or "Joint Favorable" or "JF". They may "box" the bill or defeat the bill in committee through a roll call. They may issue an unfavorable report or issue no report at all, at which the bill fails. Sometimes a committee passes a motion to give a bill a "FS" or "Favorable Substitute," which is a favorable report to a new version of a specific bill. If the bill needs action by another committee, for example, an appropriation, it goes to the Appropriations Committee. Once the bill clears all of the committees it needs to clear, it is sent to the Legislative Commissioner's Office to check for constitutionality and consistency with standing law. This is known as the first reading. The Office of Fiscal Analysis formulates an estimate of the bill's cost and the Office of Legislative Research develops an explanation of the bill. The Clerk of the House or Senate then presents the bill to its particular chamber for the second reading and then assigns a calendar number to the bill and it is printed. After the second day from when it was placed on file, the bill is ready for action. They are marked with an "XX." The bill is then read for the third time and debated in the house of origin where it could be sent back to committee. The house of origin votes on the bill and if it passes, it is sent to the other house for placement on its calendar. The other house votes on the bill and if it passes, it is sent to the Governor for signature, veto or no action. If it passed the second house with an amendment, it is returned to the first house for concurrence. If the second house cannot come to an agreement on the bill, it is sent to a joint conference committee, where, if an agreement is reached, it is sent back to both houses for either passage or rejection. If it passes and gets to the governor's office, the governor can sign the bill and it becomes law. If the governor does nothing, the bill becomes law within five days within the session or fifteen days after the legislature adjourns. If the governor vetoes the bill, the bill is sent back to the house of origin, where it may be re-passed if that house as well as the other house can reach a 2/3s majority vote to override the veto.[17] The secretary of the state, according to Article Third, Section 2 of the constitution convenes a post-adjournment or "trailer" session for actions to be taken on any vetoed bills that had not been reconsidered.

Some bills are colorfully referred to by animal names. "Cats and dogs" refer to "pet" projects that legislators support for specific groups of their constituents. A "rat" is a bill that a legislator thinks is a bad bill. Sometimes, for political reasons, a legislator may have to swallow a "rat" for political reasons.[18]

The work of the legislature results in what are called Public Acts which are laws of general applicability and which are incorporated into the Connecticut General Statutes. The legislature may also pass, Special Acts, which only affects a limited group of people and may be of limited duration. Special Acts are not incorporated into the Connecticut General Statutes, but carry the full weight of Connecticut law. The Connecticut General Statutes is the official set of published state laws. They contain fifty-five separate titles or areas of law.

Members of Connecticut's General Assembly, like members in other states' legislatures, are individuals who represent a wide range of interests, motivations, backgrounds and political opinions. Like in many other states the composition of both the lower and the upper house seems to exhibit familiar and traditional characteristics. For example, both houses continue to be dominated by male members though there has been some improvement in women representation since 1975. In that year, there were 163 men and only twenty-four women in the General Assembly. In 2002, there were 129 men and fifty-seven women in the General Assembly. This was virtually unchanged from 1999 when there were 131 men and fifty-six women. Reeher found that members of the Connecticut Senate tended to be predominantly white, Catholic, upwardly mobile, financially comfortable and well-educated.[19] In terms of occupation, more members in both houses continue to identify themselves as lawyers than any other occupation, yet there are only three women attorneys.

The motivations for seeking office in the General Assembly vary greatly. Through his interviews with Senators, a typology of legislators was formulated by Reeher that helps to explain why some individuals ran for office. There are those who sincerely want to make a difference in public policy and are perceived as the crusaders; there are those who seem to thoroughly enjoy the political process and who are perceived as the political bugs; finally there are those who seek personal gain by seeking opportunities to make money for themselves or their business.[20]

It has been found that many Connecticut legislators made the decision to run for legislative office not because of any great influence of a political party, but rather on the strength of their own initiative. Family and friends were also very important influences in their decisions to run for office.[21]

The Legislative Commissions

Beyond its responsibility for creating the laws of the state, the General Assembly staffs its own agencies that deal with several special areas of interest that enables the legislature to monitor issues and develop legislative policy. These commissions include: The Commission on Children, The Permanent Commission on the Status of Women, The Office of the Auditors of Public Accounts, The African American Affairs Commission and the Latino and Puerto Rican Affairs Commission.

The purpose of the Permanent Commission on the Status of Women, created in 1973, as stated in Connecticut General Statute 46a-4, is to be a source of information on sex discrimination and women's issues such as health, education and employment within the state for leaders in business, government and the media. It also serves to promote the consideration of qualified women for all levels of government work and oversees programs and practices in all state agencies as they affect women. In 2000, the commission received 119 requests for assistance concerning sex discrimination.[22]

The mission of The Office of the Auditors of Public Accounts is to conduct audits of all state agencies. Auditors are empowered to examine the performance and efficiency of all state agencies. Two state auditors, representing the Democrats and Republicans, are appointed by the state legislature to oversee this office.[23]

The Commission on Children is a bipartisan commission created in 1985 that oversees issues regarding children and youth. It assesses and reviews state programs affecting children, works with private providers of services to children in reviewing their concerns and works with leaders of business, government and the media to improve the delivery of services to children.[24]

The Latino and Puerto Rican Affairs Commission was created in 1994 and reviews and comments on state legislation regarding the Latino and Puerto Rican communities within Connecticut. It encourages Latino and Puerto Rican participation in government and serves to highlight the accomplishments and contributions made to the state by the Latino and Puerto Rican communities.[25]

The African-American Affairs Commission's mission is to improve the health, education political and economic conditions for African-Americans in Connecticut. It was created in 1997 and provides information and advocacy in the state legislative process. It also encourages African-American representation at all levels of state government.[26]

Lobbies in Connecticut

The primary functions of lobbies or interest groups are to influence public policy. This usually happens during the law-making process. As a consequence, at the state level of government, lobbyists spend a lot of their time speaking with lawmakers and providing them with information as to why or why not certain bills should become laws.

Former State Legislator Judge Robert Satter, described lobbies in the state in the following way, "I finally came to recognize lobbyists as a necessary part of the legislative process. The information they provided to influence my vote always had to be critically scrutinized, but it often proved to be the most helpful I received on a bill."[27]

Grant Reeher observed in his study of the Connecticut Senate, that in Connecticut, lobbies were to be found "everywhere and all the time."[28] According to Connecticut General Statute, 1-91, lobbying means "communicating directly or soliciting others to communicate with any official or his staff in the legislative or executive branch of government or in a quasi-public agency for the purpose of influencing any legislative or administrative action." There are some exceptions to this such as, communicating in a contested case, communicating as a salesperson, communications by an attorney practicing law or specific other exemptions defined under Uniform Administrative Procedures. Lobbies therefore fall into two groups: client lobbyists who wish to have their interests represented and expressed and communicator lobbyists who actually do the work of lobbying.[29] Technically, an individual who makes expenditures of $2,000 or more in any calendar year or receives compensation of $2,000 or more in any calendar year in the furtherance of lobbying is a lobbyist. Public officials acting within their official authority, publishers or owners of media acting in the normal course of their businesses, individuals representing themselves before the legislature, and United States Senators and United States Representatives, are not considered to be lobbyists. All lobbyists must register with the State Ethics Commission every two years and must file financial reports on a quarterly basis. While engaged in the lobbying process, they must wear identifying badges.

Gaining access to policy makers and hoping to be a favorable influence for their clients are critical to the lobbying process. Lobbyists attempt to do their jobs using various techniques. Publishing informational materials, giving presentations before legislative committee hearings, using a legislator's constituents to bring pressure on that legislator, wining and dining legislators or government staff people and, even on occasion, threatening legislators with electoral repercussions.[30]

Traditionally, lobbies at the state level have been involved in the areas of business, labor, education, agriculture and local government. Lobbies that have been traditionally important in Connecticut have included the insurance companies, labor, the Farm Bureau Federation and the Connecticut Manufacturers Association.[31] In 1997, it was reported that there were about 2,650 registered lobbyists in the state.[32] The interest areas with the greatest number of interest groups appear to be manufacturing, health and social services, finance and real estate, and public and consumer interest.[33]

Two widely known, respected and powerful lobbying firms presently working in the state are Gaffney, Bennett & Associates of New Britain, which in 2001 earned nearly $4 million in fees and Robinson and Cole of Hartford which earned about $1.97 million. Gaffney, Bennett and Associates represent such clients as United States Tobacco, General Electric and Yale-New Haven Hospital.[34] Other lobbies in the state include, Rome, Frankel and Kennelly which represented in 2000 such clients as:

Connecticut Association of Realtors, Inc., Mohegan Tribal Gaming Authority, and Pfizer, Inc. and Betty Gallo and Company, which in the same year, represented such clients such as the Connecticut Bar Association, the American School for the Deaf and the American Association of University Professors. The fees normally earned by lobbies can come in the form of annual fees, per session fees, retainers, per contract or per month fees. They can range from several hundred dollars a month to six figure retainers and contracts.[35] In 2001, the lobby spending the most was the Connecticut Business and Industry Association, which spent $1.2 million in lobbying activity and the media.[36]

Connecticut lobbyists, such as Patrick Sullivan and Craig LeRoy were successful in 2000 in helping to head off state legislation that would mandate stricter state emission standards for Connecticut's power plants, which have become popularly known as the "Filthy Five" or "Sooty Six". The power companies argued that the expenses that would be incurred by requiring them to retrofit their plants to achieve cleaner emissions might lead to their shutdown. State Representative Christopher Cairns of Bridgeport, who is an advocate for the clean-up law admitted at that time that the lobbies in this policy area "seem to wield a great, great deal of power in controlling the fate of this type of legislation."[37] Within two years, this power was tested. In May of 2002, with efforts from the Connecticut Coalition for Clean Air, an advocacy organization composed of about 150 diverse groups including the Bridgeport Health Improvement Project, the Green Party and the Stratford First Congregational Church, the governor signed legislation passed by tremendous majorities of both houses of the General Assembly requiring lower sulfur dioxide emissions from power plants.[38]

Most of the municipal governments in Connecticut also have their interests represented at the state level. The Connecticut Conference of Municipalities (CCM) is an organization watching out for the interests of municipal governments across the state. The CCM, founded in 1966, represents Connecticut municipalities before the legislative, executive and judicial branches of Connecticut state government. This group provides member towns with management, research, labor relations and training assistance.[39]

What's it like to be a lobbyist? Meghan Pattyson works for Roy and LeRoy, a prominent lobbying firm whose clients include Aetna, Citigroup and Philip Morris. She was also a standout member of the University of Connecticut's Women's Basketball team, graduating in 1992 and coaching there until 1995. She likens the lobbying process to a basketball season. "All the preparation at the beginning when the session first starts. How you're going along and it's not high pressure, but as the session progresses it gets a little more intricate and detail oriented. And then the last couple of weeks of the session that are kind of like the NCAA tournament, where everything comes down to this. That's when your competitive juices really get flowing. These guys live for that time."[40]

Chapter 5

The Governor and
Other Chief Executive Officers

In these difficult economic times, you can no longer "govern" a state. . . .
Politics and the two party system make "governing" impossible. Today
you don't govern, you "manage."

Lowell P. Weicker,
former Connecticut Governor[1]

The Scope of Executive Authority

The chief executive officer of the state is the governor, and as
the chief executive, the governor is in a position to exercise a wide range
of formal and informal powers. Whether as the spokesperson for the state
in welcoming back the national championship basketball team, declaring
that budget cuts in state agencies are needed to balance the state budget
or speaking with the President of the United States and other governors
about a statewide emergency such as an occurrence of anthrax, it is the
governor who commands the attention of the media and therefore, the
public. When something affecting the entire state is of concern, it is the
governor who plays the lead role.

The governor serves as the chief administrator, presiding over a
vast state bureaucracy that serves a variety of areas from the economy, the
environment, and education to health care and social services. Each one of
these areas and many more are administered by commissioners and directors picked by the governor and approved by the General Assembly.

The governor of Connecticut appoints commissioners to the following major departments:

- The Department of Administrative Services
- The Department of Agriculture
- The Department of Banking

- The Department of Children and Families
- The Department of Consumer Protection
- The Department of Correction
- The Department of Economic and Community Development
- The Department of Environmental Protection
- The Board of Higher Education
- The Department of Housing
- The Department of Insurance
- The Department of Labor
- The Department of Mental Health
- The Department of Mental Retardation
- The Department of Motor Vehicles
- The Office of Policy and Management
- The Department of Public Health and Addiction Services
- The Department of Public Safety
- The Department of Public Works
- The Department of Revenue Services
- The Department of Social Services
- The Department of Transportation
- The Department of Veteran's Affairs

According to the 2000 Census, in Connecticut, there are just under 66,000 state employees.[2] Timothy J. Moynihan, former Connecticut Democratic State Chairman, has said that the governor in effect "runs the largest business in the State of Connecticut" in terms of employees.[3] Unlike their corporate counterparts, though until recently, governors in Connecticut did their jobs for an annual salary of just $78,000. As of 2003, this was raised to $150,000. The governor's staff usually consists of an executive aide, who is the chief legislative and political advisor for the governor, a legal counsel, who reviews legislation passed by the General Assembly and advises the governor on legal matters and serves as liaison to the judicial branch, administrative aides who help the governor develop and monitor her or his programs and policies, a press secretary who coordinates media activities for the governor and an executive secretary who schedules appointments. The governor also has a military staff which consists of the adjutant general and chief of staff of the National Guard, aides-de-camp representing air, naval, marine and coast guard services, a surgeon general and the commandants of the Governor's Foot Guard and Horse Guard.

In the beginning, with no veto power and no ability to adjourn the legislature, the governor did not represent a separate branch of government. The legislature held the most significant power of government. The governor of Connecticut, at that time, served merely as a dignified head of state.[4] The Fundamental Orders required that the governors' terms ran for just one year and that they could not serve a consecutive term. Today, the formal powers of the governor of Connecticut are found in Article Fourth of the State Constitution, and they go far beyond whatever executive powers early governors could have imagined. The governor and lieutenant-governor run for statewide office as a unit and serve a four-year term. The lieutenant-governor serves as the president of the Senate and in the event that the governor dies, resigns, is removed, refuses to serve or is unable to carry out her or his executive duties, the lieutenant-governor exercises the powers of governor. The minimum age to be governor in Connecticut is thirty. The governor is the captain-general of the militia of the state except when it is called into federal service. The governor may require information from the executive agencies to carry out his duties as chief executive. The governor has the power to adjourn the General Assembly. The governor also gives the General Assembly a state of the state report. The governor of Connecticut has the power to grant a reprieve, but not a pardon. The governor can sign or veto legislation. If she or he does nothing at all to legislation, after five days it becomes law. In sum, the governor must faithfully execute all the laws of the state.

In discussing the abilities of new governors to lead their states, Thad Beyle writes that more recently it is the, "strong individual personality and the views and styles of those seeking the governorship that were critically important for winning and carrying out their duties."[5] A good example of this is Lowell P. Weicker, Jr., governor from 1991-1995. During his time as a U.S. Senator, Weicker, a Republican, earned a reputation as an independent thinker unwilling to follow the partisan crowd. In his bid for governor, he attracted the support of many unaffiliated voters. Russell D. Murphy states that the focus of his campaign "was Weicker himself and his personal qualities as a strong, no-nonsense leader."[6] Governors, therefore, must often rely on their personal skills beyond the formal powers given to them. Informally, the governor brings to the office her or his own personal talents, vision, character and personality. According to Robert Kravchuk, governors must skillfully use their formal powers "while maintaining sufficient personal prestige to remain in the game, no matter what."[7] Being a hard worker, having a sense of humor, demonstrating leadership qualities and being willing to compromise are traits that may assist governors above and beyond their formal powers. The governor may at times have highly visible ceremonial powers as the head of the state which underscores her or his role as representative of the people. The governor also is called upon to serve as the chief representative of her or his political party. On these occasions, governors must rely on personal leadership characteristics.

Any governor therefore, exercises a variety of formal and informal powers as chief executive of the state. The tasks a governor may be called upon to do are many. Charles R. Adrian has written that the governor is also "chief of state, the voice of the people, chief executive, commander in chief of the state's armed forces, chief legislator and chief of his party."[8] It will serve to help illustrate how Connecticut's governors have fulfilled these roles and exercised their power by taking a brief look at some of Connecticut's governors, past and present.

The Governor and the Budget

It is said that President Harry Truman had a sign on his desk which read, "The Buck Stops Here." The poignant message of that sign was that, when all is said and done, only the person who sat behind that desk could be responsible and make the really tough decisions. So too with governors. Some of the most challenging decisions have to do with the state's budget.

One of the chief responsibilities of governor as chief executive is the development and recommendation of the state's budget. Historically, because it is the governor who presents the executive budget to the legislature, and generally it is the legislature which responds to that budget, the governor has great influence on molding the state's budget. The governor's office has been called the "single most powerful office in the budget process."[9] Candidate for Governor Ella Grasso, friend to labor, and supporter of social programs for the elderly and disadvantaged, inherited a $70 million dollar debt from outgoing governor Thomas Meskill when she came to power in 1974.[10] Faced with the reality of a state in a fiscal crisis, Governor Grasso chose a difficult course: raise taxes and lay off state employees.[11]

In the 1970s and 1980s, the state of Connecticut operated under an annual budget. For the 1993-94 fiscal year, the state returned to a biennial budget process that it had followed in its earlier history. This process is specified in Connecticut General Statutes 4-71-4-74a. On August 1st, budget request forms and instructions from the Office of Policy and Management are sent to state agencies. After receiving biennial budget requests from the state agencies by September 1st of even-numbered years, the Office of Policy and Management sends a draft budget to the governor by November 16. The governor reviews these requests and makes her or his policy decisions. The result is called the executive budget. This budget package, containing a separate budget for each year of the biennium, outlines in detail both expenditures and revenues for the next two years and contains a report outlining estimated expenditures and revenues for the following three years. It is submitted to the General Assembly in February of each odd-numbered year. In even-numbered years, the governor submits, in February, a report on the status of the enacted budget containing any needed adjustments and a projection of expenditures and revenues for the next three years. The final state budget is adopted before the General Assembly adjourns in early June. The governor's budget is composed of four parts:

1. the budget message,
2. recommendations for appropriates for each agency for each fiscal year of the biennium, drafts of the appropriations, bonding and revenue bills needed to carry out the recommendations,
3. recommendations regarding the economy and
4. the effect of the budget on the economy.

In an effort to control state spending, a law was passed in 1991 establishing a limit on the state's general budget expenditures. This was followed by an amendment to the Connecticut Constitution adopted in 1992 which provided for a spending cap on general expenditures. The Constitutional Amendment requires that the General Assembly, by a three-fifths majority vote, adopt the necessary laws to implement the constitutional spending cap. This legislation, implementing the constitutional spending cap has not yet been passed. Thus, Connecticut has a statutory spending cap, not a constitutional one, and in the opinion of the Attorney General, the statutory cap remains in place until the General Assembly acts on the spending cap amendment. State law specifies that general budget expenditures may not exceed the previous year's expenditures by more than the average increase in personal income in the state over the past five years, determined by the U.S. Bureau of Economic Analysis or the percentage increase in inflation during the previous twelve months as determined by the United States Bureau of Labor Statistics, whichever is greater. The limit can be exceeded if the governor declares an emergency and the legislature agrees to exceed the limit by a three-fifths majority vote. (CGS Section 2-33a)

Whether or not the cap can be exceeded has caused some heated political discussion between the governor and some state legislators about the type of money that should be included under it. Depending on one's fiscal philosophy, the spending cap can be perceived as an inescapable straight jacket designed to restrain legislative spending or an effective but flexible mechanism which imposes some spending limits while allowing the legislature to address urgent state needs.[12] In Connecticut, about 80 percent of the state's budget is subject to the cap, including federal funds.[13]

A classic example of a Connecticut governor acting as Chief executive is Governor Lowell P. Weicker, Jr. and the slot machine memorandum of agreement that he signed with Skip Hayward, tribal leader of the Mashantucket Pequots. Weicker, as governor, had gone on record that he was opposed to casino gambling in Connecticut.[14] Yet despite his best efforts to organize a legislative challenge to the establishment of a casino, when the U.S. Secretary of the Interior signed the tribal-state compact in May of 1991 allowing casino gambling, it became federal law. What the tribe did not get however, with the compact, and what it desperately wanted, were slot machines which were forbidden by state law.[15]

The state's budget in 1992 was again turning up short. The tribe approached Weicker's staff and made a proposal that was hard to dismiss. The Mashantucket Pequot Tribe would give the state of Connecticut 25 percent of its casino slots winnings or a minimum of $100 million per year, whatever was greater, if the state agreed to allow slot machines in the tribe's casino and keep them illegal everywhere else. There would be no cost to the state. Weicker and Hayward signed the agreement and slot machines were available for play in January, 1993. When some of the state's legislators questioned the Governor's authority to sign such an agreement, Attorney General Richard Blumenthal pointed out that Weicker was in effect acting as chief executive in carrying out federal laws.[16] Weicker's aim was to try to get Connecticut back on track by "managing it more like a business than a state."[17] As an independent governor, with great personal and political strengths, Weicker seemed uniquely qualified to carry out this task. If the levying of an income tax and arranging a significant revenue stream from slot machines could help to bring Connecticut back out of debt, then it would be made so. Also to this end, under Weicker, a new biennial budget process was developed, an automated budget system was initiated, a program of performance measurement was put into place in state agencies, the state of information technology was reviewed and standardized and a Total Quality Management program for the state was introduced.[18]

Chief Legislator

By 1990, Connecticut had hit a bad recession and in 1992 the state budget faced a $2.4 billion shortfall. Governor Weicker promoted an income tax to address the dire fiscal situation. Utilizing his legislative powers, he vetoed the budget three times before he finally signed a progressive income tax based budget in 1991 which was linked to promoting economic development.[19] After nearly a decade of relative prosperity, Connecticut in 2001 was facing a $300 million deficit. Governor Rowland exercising his formal power called for a special session that November of the General Assembly to consider budget cuts.[20] As the year 2003 began, the state was still facing a budget crisis with the possibility of several thousand state employee lay-offs.

Chief of State

In the role of chief of state, Adrian claims that the governor serves as "a living symbol of the state."[21] A fiscal conservative, Governor Abraham Ribicoff stood for economic growth without raising taxes as a way to broaden and expand state services. To stimulate such growth, Ribicoff made a much publicized trip to California in 1955 to attract companies on the West Coast to the benefits of moving to the East.[22] In early February of 1978, Connecticut endured one of the worse blizzards in recent memory. Sizing up the severity of the storm, Governor Ella Grasso, the first woman to be elected governor of Connecticut in her own right, set up her headquarters in the State Armory and directed that all state roads be closed so that they could be cleared of snow. Straight talking, "Mother Ella," maintained a constant vigil of conditions and held frequent press briefings with the media to keep the people of Connecticut informed. Because of her sense of "riding it out" as crisis manager, while the snow piled up, the people of the state felt secure despite the worst that the storm could throw at them. Grasso's political capital, meanwhile, was also secured.[23]

Grasso's actions during the snow storm were perceived in stark contrast to the actions taken by Governor Thomas Meskill back in 1973. In December of that year, there was also a severe snowstorm. After taking all the necessary precautions, alerting the appropriate agencies and even surveying the towns suffering the most from the storm, Governor Meskill took his children on a skiing trip to Vermont. Whether or not his presence in the state would have made any difference at all, the negative image of the governor being away from a state in need left a lasting impression that was hard to live down.[24] Governor Meskill did not run for re-election.

Voice of the People

In this role, according to Adrian, the governor should articulate the aspirations and conscience of the citizens of the state.[25] Even before he became governor, Abraham Ribicoff seemed almost to be a natural in his ability to articulate the voice of the people of Connecticut. During his campaign for governor in 1954, he delivered what came to be known as the "American Dream" speech. In this speech referred to by Lieberman, Ribicoff, a Jewish candidate, said that this election would demonstrate, "whether the American dream is still alive—that any boy regardless of race, creed, or color has the right to aspire to public office. I am convinced that the heart and soul of the state of Connecticut is sound and decent and good."[26]

As governor, Ribicoff witnessed a rise in traffic fatalities in the state. He imposed stiff penalties for speeding in 1956, causing about 30,000 drivers in the state to have their licenses suspended. While the pundits claimed he would sacrifice his next election, he received tremendous popular support.[27] Grasso's plain speaking style and down to earth manner helped to influence and inspire while reminding the people of her small town roots.[28] Grasso clearly saw the job of governor as "a people's job."[29]

The Present

Full of ambition, John Rowland had been the youngest person ever elected to Congress. On January 4, 1995, John G. Roland, at 37, became the youngest governor in the history of Connecticut and the first

Republican to win the office in twenty years.[30] In his inaugural speech, Governor Rowland called for a leaner state budget, more local control for towns and cities in terms of government and education, and a tougher stand on crime.[31] During his first term, Rowland led the effort for tax cuts and welfare reform as the state's economy experienced a revitalization. A *Hartford Courant*/University of Connecticut poll in September, 1998 indicated that 73 percent of those polled thought the governor was doing an excellent or good job.[32] In his bid for re-election in 1998, Rowland, still the nation's youngest governor, was able to soundly defeat veteran Democrat Congresswoman Barbara Kennelly, daughter of former democratic party boss John Bailey.

Under Rowland, the state's six largest cities received $1.4 billion in development aid by 2000. He spearheaded a $455 million development project called Adriaen's Landing for downtown Hartford.[33] He also signed into law, UConn 2000, an ambitious program of $1 billion dollars worth of renovations and new buildings at the University of Connecticut. Rowland also undertook prison reform and welfare reform. In 2001, Governor Rowland was tapped to head the Republican Governors Association, thereby further developing his political skills and expanding his reputation beyond Connecticut.

How Governor Rowland has fulfilled some of the roles traditionally played by governors can best be illustrated by a brief review of some significant events that he has gone through during his second term of office. These are: the scandal in the State Treasurer's Office; the breakdown of the New England Patriots deal; his veto of the campaign finance reform law; how he dealt with the terrorist attacks of September 11 and the anthrax breakout in Connecticut.

Scandal in the Treasurer's Office

In 1997 when state treasurer Christopher Burnham resigned his office to pursue a more lucrative job in the private sector, Governor Rowland, exercising one of his formal powers appointed Paul Silvester as his replacement. In the 1998 election, Silvester lost a close race for treasurer to Democrat Denise Nappier. What happened after that has been subject to allegation and conjecture. According to Silvester, before he left office, he asked Rowland for perks and jobs for friends. Rowland said he could not help. Then the brother of someone close to Rowland approached Silvester and allegedly told him if he wanted the jobs, he would have to invest more state pension money in a fund in which the brother had a partnership interest. Silvester placed $25 million into the fund, three weeks before his term expired. State records revealed several of Silvester's staffers received jobs a short time later.[34] Rowland has steadfastly denied any link at all to the scandal saying no one ever had any authority to speak for him to Silvester on such questionable matters.

Special Session 2002

In FY 2001-2002, Connecticut was again facing a budget deficit due to overspending and slower than expected revenue growth. This time, the deficit was in the amount of $300 million. As chief legislator, Governor Rowland called for a Special Session of the General Assembly in November 2001, to address the budget gap. He hoped that the entire amount could be eliminated. Democrats in the General Assembly did not feel the same urgency, however, and a compromise was achieved. The special session was able to produce a compromise deficit reduction bill which reduced the deficit by $200 million. This was achieved by $136.6 million in budget cuts and savings in energy and debt service and $63.5 million from refinancing some capital projects through long term bonding.[35] This deficit represented about 2.5 percent of the state's $13 billion budget. While Senator Louis C. DeLuca said that the compromise plan merely pushed Connecticut's financial problems into the future, Governor Rowland demonstrated his flexibility and was more satisfied, saying, "I'll take two-thirds of a loaf any day." [36]

Catching the Pass, But Out of Bounds

When the NHL Hartford Whalers left Connecticut for economic reasons, many sports fans in the state missed their outlet for locally following the highest level of professional sports competition. When NFL New England Patriots owner Robert Kraft began to think of moving his team, he found Governor Rowland, a former high school wrestler, and who was developing an urban agenda which included major development plans in Hartford, a ready and willing partner. As lead spokesman for the state, Rowland met with Kraft behind the scenes to hammer out a deal that would essentially have the state of Connecticut build the Patriots a new stadium in Hartford. As chief legislator, Rowland called for a special session of the General Assembly in December of 1998 where a stadium bill which authorized the construction of a $374 million stadium readily passed.[37] Despite the tremendous energy, effort and optimism the governor demonstrated publicly for the stadium project, in the end, Robert Kraft backed away and the deal fell through. A combination of underestimated preparation problems at the stadium site which would delay its opening, the negative influence exerted by the NFL commissioner in telling Kraft that Hartford would be a poor alternative as a relocation site, and the Massachusetts legislature coming up with their own plans to build a new stadium for the Patriots spelled disaster for the Governor's desire for a Connecticut professional football team. The deal, which had sparked the imagination of most of the state and which might have changed the face of the state capitol and enhanced the lives of those who live in it, was called off on April 30, 1999. For the governor, it probably turned out for the best. A Quinnipiac College Poll begun just before the announcement of the failed deal found that 58 percent of Connecticut residents polled were somewhat or strongly opposed to the Patriot's deal and had revealed that the governor's job performance rating was falling. After the announcement that the deal was off, his job approval ratings stopped falling.[38]

Campaign Finance Reform

Since taking office in 1994, Governor Rowland signed nine pieces of legislation into law concerning campaign finance reform.[39] In 2000, both houses of the General Assembly passed a bill entitled, *An Act Proposing Comprehensive Finance Reform for Statewide Constitutional Offices*. This bill would have established voluntary spending limits for candidates for statewide offices in 2002 and legislative offices in 2004, create a Citizen's Election Fund to collect money to pay for campaigns and would also limit the amount of money individuals and business PACs could contribute to candidates for constitutional offices.[34]

Acting in the role of chief legislator, Governor Rowland vetoed this bill. He gave six main reasons for his decision:

1. The bill was not bipartisan and was not a product of bipartisan deliberation. Democratic legislators mostly favored it, Republicans disapproved.

2. The bill did not incorporate recommendations for reform given by the State Election Enforcement and State Election Commissions such as restricting the number of PACs a person or entity could maintain to only one.

3. The bill imposed arbitrary spending limits for candidates.

4. The bill did not restrict the involvement of special interests in elections.

5. The bill takes money away from other programs to fund campaigns and imposes arbitrary spending limits.

6. Finally, there was a question of whether the bill imposed restrictions on candidate's First Amendment rights to freely engage in political speech.[41]

His veto was not overridden.

Terror Strikes Connecticut

In the wake of the terrorist attacks of September 11, all across America people felt the threat of unknown dangers and state governors responded as chief executives and commanders of their state's militias. Connecticut's proximity to New York City in particular left a special sadness in the aftermath of the attacks as a significant number of Connecticut citizens were killed in the World Trade Center. After a conference call with Director of Homeland Security Tom Ridge in which all states participated, Governor Rowland, as captain general, ordered the National Guard to patrol the state's nuclear power facilities, ordered the state police to a state of high alert, ordered the state Department of Environmental Protection to assist the Coast Guard with twenty-four hour marine patrols, and ordered the State Office of Emergency Management to also be staffed twenty-four hours a day.[42] As Chief of State, Governor Rowland acted as only he could have under such circumstances, on the night of the attacks, he journeyed down to the Stamford train station and offered his greetings and sympathies to those commuters returning to their homes from their jobs in New York City. In the days following the disaster, Governor Rowland quietly called all the Connecticut victims' families to offer his sorrow and extend any needed state services to them.[43] When a case of anthrax popped up in the state, killing a ninety-four year old woman in November, 2001, as the voice of the people, he urged the citizens of Connecticut to "Go on living your lives, don't live in fear."[44]

Despite enduring criticism as being a "chameleon" on certain issues, having a deal to bring the New England Patriots to Hartford reneged on by Robert Kraft and having endorsed a treasurer saddled with a scandal that led to his resignation and indictment, Governor Rowland has continued to prove his resilience. According to Morton Tenzer, Professor Emeritus of political science at the University of Connecticut, Governor Rowland "has been connected to the kinds of scandals that could have ruined other governors."[45] He has also continued to be a popular governor. This is at least in part, due to his sense of humor and ability to charm an audience.[46] In March of 2001, the governor was quoted in *The Hartford Courant* is a feature article about snowstorms and politics. "You can screw up the budget", said Rowland, "but don't ever mess up a snowstorm."[47] This is also how much of the state's population sees him. According to Dean Pagani, spokesman for the governor, "The people of Connecticut recognize the governor as someone who comes in every day and works hard, regardless of what the job throws at him."[48] A Quinnipiac College Poll in February 2002 gave him an approval rating of 65 percent.[49] In the 2002 gubernatorial race, Governor Rowland ran for a rare third term against a familiar Democratic adversary, William Curry, a former state comptroller who was seeking the governorship for a second time. Throughout the campaign season, Governor Rowland consistently enjoyed a double digit lead in the opinion polls. On November 5, 2002, John Rowland became Governor for the third time, and if he completes his term, with twelve years in office, he will have been the longest serving governor in Connecticut since Jonathan Trumbull, who served from 1769-1784.

Other Executive Officers

While the governor may be referred to as the chief executive of the state, as Robert Lorch writes, in most states, there are several executive level officers who independently run in statewide elections and share executive power, thus providing within the state, a plural executive. They may even be of different political parties than the governor.[50] In Connecticut, elected in their own right in statewide elections are the Attorney General, Treasurer, Comptroller, and Secretary of the State. These are the Constitutional officers and together with the Governor, make up the state's executive officers.

Attorney General

The Connecticut General Assembly created the Office of Attorney General in 1897. The attorney general, as chief legal officer of the state, supervises all legal matters in which the state is an interested party, except in legal matters over which prosecuting attorneys have jurisdiction. The attorney general appears for the state, governor, lieutenant-governor, the secretary of the state, the treasurer, comptroller, department heads, state boards, commissioners and many more state officers. The attorney general gives her or his opinion on questions of law when requested by either house of the General Assembly, the president pro tempore of the Senate, the speaker of the House and majority or minority leaders in either house. In the past, attorney Richard Blumenthal, the current attorney general, has released the names of dead beat parents owing child support money, has monitored developments with the federal Bureau of Indian Affairs on tribal recognition in Connecticut, and has jointed other states in suing RJR Tobacco Company for continuing to market its products to youths by placing adds in magazines with significant youthful readership.[51] While this officer has no jurisdiction in criminal matters, graft and corruption in the state can be investigated.

Comptroller

The state comptroller oversees the keeping of all public accounts of the state. It was created in 1786 by the General Assembly. To this end, the Comptroller prepares all financial accounting statements of the state and pays all wages and salaries of state employees. This office is responsible for examining all invoices and purchase orders relating to the state. The Office administers all Retirement Systems with the exception of the Teacher's Retirement System. The comptroller's office also gives a monthly accounting of the state's financial condition.[52]

Treasurer

The treasurer receives all monies belonging to the state as custodian, invests state funds and makes disbursements according to law. The state treasurer is responsible for cash management and issuance of state bonds. The Treasurer makes an annual report to the Governor concerning the receipts and expenditures of the State for the fiscal year.[53] According to former Connecticut Treasurer Christopher B. Burnham, Connecticut's treasury, "has been like a large global investment bank. With a staff of almost 200, banking relationships in a dozen countries and dealings with more than 500 financial institutions on Wall Street and around the world, the Office of the Treasurer manages billions of dollars in cash and cash flow and nearly $20 billion in pension funds. . . ."[54]

Secretary of the State

The secretary of the state is the official keeper of the state's public documents and records. The secretary of the state receives all public and special acts passed by the legislature and transmits them to the governor and then records the executive action. The secretary of the state is also responsible for maintaining all records that are by law required to be filed by corporations within the state. In recent years, the Secretary of the State has played a leadership role in citizenship education. The office has six divisions including an Elections Division which administers state and local election laws and a Commercial Recording Division, which is responsible for the administration of laws governing limited liability, certificates of incorporation, merger and dissolution. The State Board of Accountancy, which insures that the standards of professionalism are maintained by Connecticut's Certified Public Accountants is administered from this Office. The secretary of the state's Office also oversees the publication of the *State Register and Manual* and other handbooks concerning election laws. Before she became governor, Democrat Ella Grasso was Secretary of the State. Pauline Kezer, Republican, made great progress in raising awareness of the importance of democratic participation in the state, but despite an energetic campaign, was unable to turn her experience as secretary into a successful bid for the governor's office.

CHAPTER 6

Connecticut's Judicial Branch

An independent and honorable judiciary is indispensable to justice in our society.

Connecticut Code of Judicial Conduct, Canon 1 [1]

Because we, as individuals with a multitude of differences live together in a basically liberal and democratic society, there are bound to be conflicts and controversies about how we get along. When we are unable to settle our differences ourselves in an orderly and peaceful fashion, we have a judicial system for the redress of our grievances, the resolution of our disputes and to determine the guilt or innocence of those accused of criminal wrongs committed against us. Our judicial system also helps to interpret our constitution and body of laws when legal questions arise.[2]

Every state in effect has two judicial systems; the federal and the state. Which system is utilized depends on the nature of the dispute or crime encountered. Federal courts appropriately have jurisdiction over such matters as disputes involving two different states or the citizens of two different states; a state and another country, cases involving diplomatic personnel, cases in which the United States is a party and matters of federal law. Connecticut courts are described under Article Fifth of the State Constitution as amended. State courts appropriately hear cases involving most other things such as contracts, personal injuries, various civil disputes and most criminal matters arising within the state.[3]

Early Courts in Connecticut

Under the Fundamental Orders, the General Court initially acted as the primary judicial authority in Connecticut. It soon established the Particular Court as the main judicial body in 1638. The Particular Court was superceded by the Court of Assistants in 1665 and the County Courts in 1666. In 1698 separate probate courts were created to handle wills and estates.[4] In 1711, the Court of Assistants was abolished and was replaced by the Superior Court. In 1784 local matters were heard by newly established city courts and the Supreme Court of Errors was created. With the Constitution of 1818, a fully separated judicial branch was established. This new constitution established a Supreme Court of Errors, a Superior Court and such lesser courts as were deemed necessary by the General Assembly. In 1855 County courts were abolished and the superior courts assumed their functions with enhanced authorities. As more towns became incorporated , local Justices of the Peace were authorized to hear small cases as trial justices in town and borough courts created by the General Assembly. The first juvenile courts were established in 1921. In 1941, a single Court of Common Pleas was established by state law to hear all civil cases. With the abolition of county government in 1960, the municipal and local trial courts were replaced by a statewide circuit court system, maintained by the state. By the end of 1974, the Circuit Court was merged with the Court of Common Pleas and in 1978, the Court of Common Pleas and the Juvenile Court merged with the Superior Court which now had become the sole trial court of general jurisdiction.[5]

The history of Connecticut's judicial system reveals that it has evolved from a rather fragmented system of circuit, municipal, common pleas and county courts to a relatively streamlined and unified statewide system.[6] As it currently stands, this system is composed of probate courts, a Superior Court of original jurisdiction, the Appellate Court and the State's Supreme Court.

Probate Court

The probate court is a court of limited jurisdiction. Its primary function is to have jurisdiction over the estates of deceased persons. The court ensures by order and decree that an orderly settlement of these estates occurs. The court also has jurisdiction over adoptions, commitment of the mentally ill, guardians of the persons and estates of minors, conservators and testamentary trusts.[7] While many of Connecticut's towns and cities have their own probate court, some of the smaller municipalities share one. By state law, the state has been divided up into 132 probate districts. Each probate district has one judge, who must be an elector of a town within the district and is elected for a four-year term. Probate judges do not have to be trained as attorneys. They earn their pay through the collection of court fees. Orders or decrees from the Probate court may be appealed to the Superior Court.

Superior Court

All cases except those coming from probate court originate in Superior Court, which has the authority to hear and decide legal controversies and promulgate its own rules of practice and procedure. Superior Court is the main trial court in Connecticut. It is also the main court of jury trials. In Connecticut, juries are randomly chosen from voter registration and motor vehicle operators' lists. Generally, those who work full-time and are called to jury service receive their regular pay from their employers for the first five days of jury service and reimbursement for necessary expenses.[8]

Superior Court is divided into four main trial divisions: civil, criminal, family and housing. According to Connecticut General Statute, 51-344, the state is broken up administratively into twelve judicial districts, twenty-two geographical area courts and fourteen juvenile districts. Major criminal and civil cases generally come before the judicial district courts. Other cases are heard at the geographical area and juvenile courts in appropriate locations.[9]

TABLE 6.1
Superior Court Caseload for Felonies and Torts: 1991-2000

	1991	1992	1993	1994	1995	1996	1997	1998	1999	2000
Felony	4,684	4,102	3,610	3,848	3,829	3,614	3,377	3,074	3,279	2,864
Tort	16,266	16,250	15,947	15,642	17,932	19,211	19,903	20,036	18,887	18,506

Source: National Center for State Courts. State Court Caseload Statistics, 2001.

Table 6.1 reveals two areas of case filings within the judicial branch during the 1990s. While the number of felonious, or serious criminal case filings decreased during the decade, the number of tort filings, or civil harms such as malpractice and accidents, rose substantially in the 1990s and only started to decline in the last two years of the decade.[10]

Civil Division

The civil division is composed of five parts, each having a specific type of case that is heard. These are:
- Part H Landlord-tenant disputes, including summary process;
- Part S Small claims;
- Part A Administrative Appeals;
- Part J Civil jury;
- Part C Civil non-jury.

These courts hear such cases as accidents, breaches of contract, and product liability. In civil cases, the person making the complaint is called the plaintiff and the person against whom the complaint is made is the defendant. Cases in this division are settled according to the standard of the preponderance of evidence.

Criminal Division

The commission or omission of an act that is in violation of a public law is a crime. In a criminal case, in theory, it is the people who have been aggrieved and the state represents them in bringing an action, in court, against the one who committed a wrong against society. Table 6.2 reveals that the overall trend in Connecticut between 1991 and 2000 has been a decrease in the number of crimes committed.[11]

Table 6.2   Comparing the Number of Offenses for Selected Crimes in 1991 and 2000

Crime	1991	2000
Arson	1,144	780
Murder	187	98
Rape	964	668
Robbery	7,394	3,852
Aggravated Assault	9,308	6,642
Burglary	39,344	17,509
Larceny	93,562	68,399
Motor Vehicle Theft	26,254	13,130

Source: Annual Report of the Uniform Crime Reporting Program, *Crime in Connecticut 2000*, State of Connecticut, Department of Public Safety, Division of State Police.

In Connecticut, the state is represented by a prosecutor who is called a state's attorney. These prosecutors carry out their duties under the authority of the Chief State's Attorney within the Division of Criminal Justice as part of the executive branch. In Connecticut, this is an entirely different jurisdiction separate from the Attorney General, who is an independently elected constitutional officer having jurisdiction in civil matters. Connecticut's prosecutors were historically part of the judicial branch but, in 1984, a state constitutional amendment transferred the prosecuting authority into the executive branch, establishing the Division of Criminal Justice. This amendment also established an independent Criminal Justice Commission which is composed of six members appointed by the governor and confirmed by the state legislature. This commission is responsible for selecting prosecutors based upon merit. There are presently over 225 state prosecutors.[12]

Chapter 952, Section 53 of the Connecticut General Statutes lists the Penal Code Offenses for the state. Within this chapter are found essentially two classifications of crime in Connecticut; felonies and misdemeanors. Felonies are crimes that carry a penalty of more than one year in prison. Misdemeanors are crimes that generally carry a punishment of less than one year in prison. These cases are heard in the criminal division, which is made up of four parts, A, B, C, and D. Here, criminal trials are assigned a part according to the severity of the crime.[13]

Part A courts deal with the worst felonies. These are crimes that are punishable by prison sentences with over twenty years. Examples include capital felony of which nine forms are recognized:

1. murder of a police officer;
2. murder for payment;
3. murder by someone who was previously convicted of murder;
4. murder by a person serving a life imprisonment;
5. murder of a kidnapped person;
6. murder caused by the sale of drugs to someone who dies of their use;
7. murder committed in the course of a sexual assault;
8. murder of two or more persons at the same time; and
9. murder of a person under 16 years old.

Part B courts deal with class B felonies and unclassified felonies punishable by sentences of ten to twenty years. Examples here may include manslaughter, and motor vehicle theft and certain drug offenses and aggravated sexual assault.

Part C courts deal with class C felonies and unclassified felonies punishable by prison terms of five to ten years. Examples here include: burglary in the second degree, sexual assault in the second degree, and promoting prostitution in the second degree.

Part D courts deal with class D felonies, misdemeanors, violations and infractions. Infractions may be minor offenses such as traffic violations. This part hears such cases as criminal trespass, minor larceny, criminal impersonation, and cheating.

While certain crimes may carry standard punishments, sometimes a judge may get creative with the punishments that he or she may hand out. Judge Howard Scheinblum is a judge with a tough and well-respected reputation within the criminal division. He tries to see every defendant brought before him as an individual and makes the effort to impose a sentence that will have some meaning for the person convicted. Among other unusual sentences, he has sent an animal abuser to work in a dog pound, and required two young men who were convicted of a hate crime to read, William Shirer's *The Rise and Fall of the Third Reich* and take a course in comparative religion.[14]

Housing Division

When there are disputes between landlords and tenants, they are settled in Part H, the Housing Division. Housing matters are defined by Connecticut General Statute 47a-68. These include evictions and small claims. This Division holds sessions in the Bridgeport, Hartford, New Haven, Stamford-Norwalk and Waterbury judicial districts.

Family Division

This Division hears cases concerning child custody, relief from abuse, family support payments and divorce. The Division also hears juvenile matters which concern children under age sixteen. Part J may include; child abuse and neglect, delinquency and termination of parental rights. Part S is concerned with support and paternity actions. Part D includes dissolution of marriage and all other family relations matters.[15]

Appellate Court

The Appellate Court was created in 1983 by a constitutional

amendment (Article XX of the Amendments) to help handle the ever growing case load of cases in Connecticut that were coming up for appeal.
This court hears appeals coming from the Superior Courts throughout the
state. The Appellate Court does not look to establish new facts. The Appellate Court is primarily concerned with ensuring that proper judicial
procedure was followed by the lower courts and that laws were properly
applied. There are nine Appellate Court judges of which three usually
hear the cases that are brought before them. One Appellate Court judge is
designated as the Chief Judge by the Chief Justice. The Appellate Court
is located in Hartford. Decisions rendered by this court may be appealed
to the Supreme Court only if that court grants certification to hear the
case.

Supreme Court

The highest court in the state of Connecticut is the Supreme Court.
It is composed of one Chief Justice and six associate justices. A panel of
five judges usually hears and decides cases, but on occasion for a case of
considerable importance, the Chief Justice calls for all of the justices to
sit and hear a case, en banc. Like the Appellate court below it, the Supreme Court reviews the cases that come before it to determine if legal
errors have been made in the lower courts. In some cases appeals may be
brought directly to the Supreme Court, without a hearing by the Appellate Court. Examples of such cases might be a case where the Superior
Court has determined that the state constitution or a state statute contains
an invalid provision or a conviction of a capital felony, certain cases involving elections, judicial conduct and any other serious case with public
impact.[16]

How Connecticut Judges are Appointed

For the appointment of judges, Connecticut basically follows a
variation of the Missouri Plan, a system of selecting judges where selection is based upon merit. All judges to the Supreme Court, the Appellate
Court and Superior Court are nominated by the governor from a list of
qualified judge candidates that is created by the twelve-member Judicial
Selection Commission. Six members of this commission are appointed
by the governor and six members are appointed by the leadership of the
General Assembly. The appointees are to be both attorneys and non-attor-

neys and no more than six can be of the same political party. Once nominated, the candidates are confirmed by the General Assembly. Judges to
these courts must be admitted to practice law in Connecticut. Their term
is eight years and they can be reappointed. Judges retire at age seventy,
after which, they become state referees for the remainder of their term.
As referees, they remain eligible for reappointment as referees for the
rest of their lives.[17] With the exception of those that are elected, judges
can be removed or suspended by the Supreme Court. Through Article
Ninth of the Constitution, judges can also be impeached by the House of
Representatives of the General Assembly and tried by the Senate. Concurrence of two-thirds of the senate is required for conviction. Through
Article Fifth of the Constitution and Article Eleventh of the Amendments
to the Constitution, judges can also be removed by the governor on direction of two-thirds of the members of the General Assembly or by the
Supreme Court.[18]

As Table 6.3 reveals, as of 2000, there were 175 judges within
the state court system.[19]

Table 6.3 Connecticut Courts: Number of Judges and Workload

Year	Number of Judges	Judges per 1,000 Population	Filings per Judge
2000	175	5.1	1,664
1999	170	5.2	1,753
1998	167	5.1	1,845

Source: National Center for State Courts: 1998, 1999, 2000

Judges in Connecticut are required to follow a Code of Judicial
Conduct, which was adopted by judges of the Superior Court in 1974.
This code is comprised of seven canons adopted by the American Bar
Association in 1972. These canons are:

1. A judge should uphold the integrity and independence of
   the judiciary.

2. A judge should avoid impropriety and the appearance of
   impropriety in all the judge's activities.

3. A judge should perform the duties of judicial office impar-
   tially and diligently.

4. A judge may engage in activities to improve the law, the legal system and the administration of justice.

5. A judge should regulate the judge's extra-judicial activities to minimize the risk of conflict with his or her judicial duties.

6. A judge should regularly file reports of compensation received for quasi-judicial and extra-judicial activities.

7. A judge should refrain from political activity inappropriate to the judicial office.[20]

Some Recent Supreme Court Cases

For years, Greenwich Point could only be enjoyed by those who were legal residents of the Town of Greenwich. In *Leydon v. Greenwich*, (2001) the State Supreme Court found that the Town of Greenwich could no longer prevent non-residents from using a town park which has a beach. Citing the First Amendment of the United States Constitution, the Court found that as a public park, it must be open to freedom of association. Under Connecticut's Constitution, freedom of association is also guaranteed and the activities of expression and association by non-residents cannot be barred on any publicly owned property so long as that activity is compatible with the normal use of that property.[21]

In *State v. Troupe*, (1996) the State Supreme Court modified its rule permitting constancy of accusation testimony in cases of sexual assault. Before this case, prosecutors were allowed to introduce into evidence detailed testimony from witnesses to whom the victim had reported the assault to corroborate the victim's testimony and to show constancy in the victim's declarations. The idea was that if the victim did not complain soon after the commitment of the crime, then the crime itself was suspect. This testimony was helpful in establishing the victim's credibility. The court found that its then current doctrine was broader than necessary. It wished to restrict the evidence gained through this type of testimony to the fact and timing of the victim's complaint, not the details.[22]

In 1997 in *Charles v. Charles*, the Supreme Court ruled that a Native American tribal member could be sued in state court. Marilyn Charles wanted to divorce her husband, Owen Charles who was a member of the Mashantucket Peaquot tribe. The superior court had ruled that because Charles had lived on the reservation, a sovereign nation, the state did not have jurisdiction. The Supreme Court ruled that tribal consent was not required to confer state jurisdiction over a civil action against a tribal member residing on the reservation. The tribe as a sovereign entity is still immune from state lawsuits.[23] In May 2001, the State Supreme court ruled in *Town of Orange v. Modern Cigarette Inc.* that the Town of Orange could impose an outright ban on cigarette vending machines within town under its municipal police powers to protect the health, safety and welfare of its citizens. The Modern Cigarette vending company challenged the local ban raised in 1998 claiming that it had a state license to operate such machines throughout the state. The Court found that there was nothing in the law regulating cigarette vending machines from limiting a town or municipality from imposing more restrictive conditions upon these types of machines.[24]

Chapter 7

Connecticut's Local Governments

*These wards, called townships in New England are the vital principal of
their governments and have proved themselves the wisest invention ever
devised by the wit of man for the perfect exercise of self government, and
for its preservation.*

Thomas Jefferson[1]

If the residents of any state were to consider which level of government within America's federal system that they most interact with on the most frequent basis, the local level must surely be the conclusion they reach. Most of us attended or send our children to local public schools, we drive our cars on roads that are maintained by local street crews, we pay local taxes on the real and personal property we own, such as our houses and cars, and when we call for help, it is usually a local fire company or police department that responds. When we vote, no matter if it is for president, governor, or mayor, we vote locally at a polling place that is administered by local voting officials.

Within the state of Connecticut, as Figure 7.1 reveals, there are 169 local, town and city governments, each reflecting their own unique character. Yet, when we examine them in terms of how they are governed we can make two basic observations. First, we find that they all share in a common basic relationship to the state of Connecticut. Second, we find that while different in terms of population, region, demographics, geography, culture, and partisanship, all of the 169 local governments in the state assume one of three basic forms of government, or a close variation of them.

Table 7.2 demonstrates that Connecticut has a very small group of large cities. Most towns and cities in the state are under 30,000 in population.[2] Yet whether large or small, most municipalities share the same concerns. All 169 towns and cities rely on the property tax to pro-

Figure 7.1 Connecticut Municipalities by County

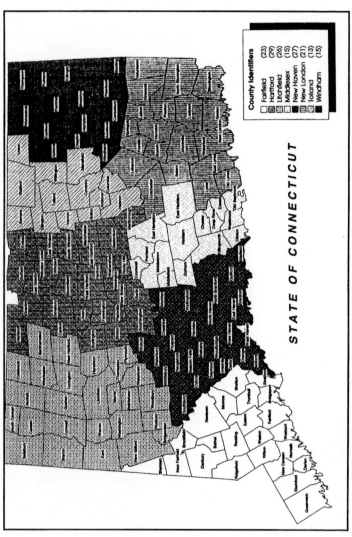

(Source: Connecticut Office of Policy and Management, Municipal Fiscal Indicators December, 1998)

Table 7.1 Connecticut Averages by Municipal Population

POPULATION	Over 70,000	30,000-70,000	10,000-30,000	Under 10,000
Number of Towns	7	22	62	78
Average School Enrollment	16,763	7,057	3,105	879
Equalized Net Grand List	$5,954,381,589	$4,051,972,071	$1,751,267,100	$467,582,878
Property Tax Revenue	$149,725,327	$72,138,839	$29,489,323	$7,855,015
Property Tax as a % of Total Revenue	52.6	68.5	69.9	70.4
Total Expenditures	$270,811,358	$101,938,630	$40,500,105	$10,704,755
Educational Expenditures	$127,241,307	$57,246,413	$25,343,669	$7,255,451
Educational Expenditures as a % of Total Expenditures	45	54.4	60.5	65.1

Source: State of Connecticut, Municipal Fiscal Indicators, 1995-1999. Office of Policy and Management. October, 2000.

vide over one-half of their revenues. All except the largest cities spend over one-half of their total expenditures on education.

The Relationship Between State and Local Government in Connecticut

The United States government is referred to as a federal republic. This essentially means that we, the people, democratically elect others to represent us within two levels of government; the state and the nation. In theory, each level enjoys its own sovereignty, with each level having certain powers and authority to act on its own behalf. Technically, federalism does not address sub-state or local governments nor does the United States Constitution specifically mention local government. The relationship between the state and local levels of government is a unitary one. The state government acts directly upon its local governments and retains its sovereignty over local affairs. This concept became referred to as the creature theory of government and it became judicial doctrine through a United States Supreme Court case called *Worcester v. Worcester Consolidated Railway Company*. (196 U.S. 539, 1905). In this case the Supreme Court said:

> A municipal corporation is simply a political subdivision of the state and exists by virtue of the exercise of the power of the state through its legislative department. The legislature could at any time terminate the existence of the corporation itself, and provide other and different means for the government of the district comprised within the limits of the former city. The city is the creature of the state.[3]

In Connecticut, the "creature" concept has even a longer history. In *Willard v. Warden*[4] the Court wrote that, "the borough and the town are. . .inferior corporations. They act not by any inherent right of legislation, like the legislature of the state, but their authority is delegated." In *Willimantic School Society v. First School Society in Windham*,[5] the state's highest court referred to towns as, "mere organs of the state." In *State Ex. Rel. Bulkeley v. Williams*[6], the court stated, "Towns have no inherent rights. They have always been the mere creatures of the Colony of the state, with such functions and such only as were conceded or recognized by law."

Over a century ago, John Forest Dillon, chief justice of the Iowa Supreme, formulated a doctrine of interpreting local law that would eventually become widely known as Dillon's Rule. Judge Dillon sat on the bench at a time in American history where there was rampant corruption in big city government. He did not place much trust in municipal government. According to his interpretation of municipal power, he felt that if there was any doubt about whether a municipality had a certain power, the doubt itself was enough for him to assume that it did not in fact have that power. In the case, *City of Clinton v. Cedar Rapids and Missouri River Rail Road Company*,[7] Dillon argued that municipal government could exercise only three kinds of power: powers expressly granted or written down within the law, powers implied by or incidental to the expressed powers and powers essential and indispensable to the objectives and purposes of the municipal corporation.[8]

In Connecticut, as well as in other states, the response to the strict interpretation of Dillon's Rule and the "creature" concept has been home rule. With the "creature" concept, local governments enjoyed virtually no flexibility on local issues. State legislatures became mediators and referees in settling local laws and as a result became bogged down with locally focused special legislation. Under the concept of home rule, some autonomy and independence is given from the state to the local government through the development and adoption of a local charter. Instead of preventing a town or city from doing anything not specifically authorized, home rule permits a city or town to do things not specifically prohibited. The state legislature, under home rule, is placed under a greater degree of restraint.

In Connecticut, home rule efforts began in 1915. This first state effort, however, ended in failure. It required that 60 percent of the local registered voters pass the proposed home rule charter. While this hurdle proved insurmountable, its significance lies in the fact that it represented the ability of municipalities to initiate the charter adoption process without first having to go to the General Assembly. Home rule was again tried in 1951, and 1953 requiring 51 percent and 26 percent respectfully, of the locally registered voters for approval. They also failed in easily enabling towns to adopt local charters. But by this time, the home rule movement was gathering momentum.[9]

In 1957 there was the passage of the Home Rule Act which outlined a specific process for local charter adoption in which a municipality could determine on its own, its form of government. In 1965, home rule was given further support with the adoption of the new state Constitution. Article Tenth of the state Constitution is the home rule article. Home rule is often discussed as either constitutional home rule or legislative home rule. Constitutional home rule is thought to be "self-executing" in that it does not require any action by the legislature for implementation. It follows that this type of home rule may be considered to be very powerful, as a constitutional amendment would be required to change or alter it. Legislative home rule on the other hand, is home rule that is authorized by statutes enacted by the state legislature. Under this view, it follows then that the legislature may be able to change the statutes far more easily.[10]

It has been said that Connecticut has what is called, "non-self-executing constitutional home rule."[11] What does this mean? Article Tenth of the state constitution states that,

> . . .the general assembly shall enact no special legislation relative to the powers, organization, terms of elective offices or form of government of any single town, city or borough, except as to (a) borrowing power, (b) validating acts and (c) formation, consolidation or dissolution of any town, city or borough, unless in the delegation of legislative authority by general law the general assembly shall have failed to prescribe the powers necessary to effect the purpose of such special legislation.

Horton says that this provision essentially only prevents the General Assembly from passing legislation that is aimed at a purely local concern. Using the case of *Shelton v. Commissioner of the Department of Environmental Protection.*[12] for illustration, he argues that if a specific local concern, for example, solid waste, also happens to be a statewide concern, then the legislature could in fact properly intervene.[13] Decisions like this have prompted some commentators to contend that the home rule powers of municipalities in Connecticut are very limited. Hollister argues that, "The statutes delegating home rule powers are often so vague as to be useless, or so specific as to provide towns no real authority to act in many areas in which they might take the lead in formulating public policy."[14] Cross says that, "In cases where the town powers are clearly defined, we see that both the General Assembly and the Supreme Court are prepared to step in to deny their use where the municipal action is repugnant to what are regarded as broader state needs or public policy."[15]

Chapter 98 of the Connecticut General Statutes has been referred to as the Home Rule Chapter. In Section 7-148, about 100 municipal powers, given to both chartered and non-chartered municipalities are enumerated. The following is a simplified summary of many of these powers. Some may be obvious and some might come as somewhat of a surprise.

Municipalities have the powers under Title 7 to:

1. Contract, sue and be sued.
2. Provide authentication and execution of deeds.
3. Establish a budget system.
4. Assess, levy and collect taxes.
5. Make appropriations and pay debts.
6. Make appropriations for public emergencies.
7. Make appropriations for hospitals and health care facilities.
8. Make contracts for unusual expenditures.
9. Provide procedures for taking land for public use.
10. Provide bonding for municipal officials.
11. Regulate methods for borrowing money.
12. Provide for the temporary borrowing of money.
13. Provide for special funds or trust funds.
14. Provide for tax liens.
15. Take or acquire property.
16. Provide for administering gifts.
17. Provide for police protection.
18. Provide fire protection.
19. Provide for entertainment.
20. Provide for ambulance service.
21. Provide for the employment of nurses.
22. Provide for the lighting of streets.
23. Provide water.
24. Provide for the collection of waste and trash.
25. Provide for low income housing.
26. Provide for a pension system.
27. Establish a merit system for employment.
28. Provide for salary and hours of employment.
29. Provide for a municipal historian.
30. Establish and construct public facilities.

31. Provide for public improvements.

32. Enter lands to survey and map.

33. Regulate and protect public buildings.

34. Provide shade trees.

35. Provide for waterfront improvement.

36. Provide for sewers and drainage.

37. Enter land to correct flow of water.

38. Regulate the laying of pipes and wires.

39. Prohibit the discharge of drains into public places.

40. Layout and construct highways and sidewalks.

41. Keep streets safe.

42. Control excavation of streets.

43. Regulate excavation of sidewalks.

44. Require owners of land adjacent to walks to remove snow.

45. Grant limited leasehold agreements to property owners.

46. Make rules for safe and sanitary housing.

47. Regulate building use.

48. Regulate the moving of buildings.

49. Regulate parked trailers.

50. Establish lines beyond which buildings cannot be built.

51. Regulate signs.

52. Regulate plumbing.

53. Regulate the construction of dwellings.

54. Regulate the speed of vehicles.

55. Regulate cesspools, drains and barns.

56. Regulate traffic.

57. Regulate animals.

58. Regulate keeping wild or domestic animals.

59. Prohibit nuisances.

60. Keep streets free of noise and nuisances.

61. Prohibit loitering on private property.

62. Prohibit nighttime loitering on public property.

63. Prevent trespassing.

64. Prevent vice.

65. Regulate shows, processions, and parades.

66. Regulate trade, business and professions as to public health.

67. Regulate auctions and tag sales.

68. License and regulate peddlers.

69. Regulate swimming.

70. Regulate amusement parks.

71. Regulate sports, exhibitions and performances.

72. Preserve public space.

73. Establish a system to record births, marriages and deaths.

74. Control insects and pests.

75. Provide for the health of inhabitants.

76. Regulate the use of streets and public places.

77. Make and enforce police regulations.

78. Regulate the calling of emergency messages.

79. Regulate and prevent housing blight.

80. Provide for the protection of the environment.

81. Regulate the location of manure and dead animals.

82. Regulate land filling.

83. Regulate the emission of smoke from any chimney.

Title 7, of the Connecticut General Statutes guarantees a selectman-town meeting form of government for every town or city in the state. Therefore, if a town does not have its own charter specifying a particular form of government, the state provides the selectman/town meeting form. Under this form of government, there is a three-person board of selectman. The First Selectman, is one of the three on the board, but serves as the chief executive officer of the town. The town meeting acts as the legislative body and must, by law meet once a year to pass the town budget and other items presented for vote. If a town wishes to change its form of government from selectman/town meeting to something else, such as a mayor-council or council-manager form, Connecticut General Statutes 7-188-191 concisely outlines the process for adopting a charter through home rule.

The Charter Process

Black's Law Dictionary defines charter as: "an instrument emanating from a sovereign power, in the nature of a grant, either to the whole nation, or to a class or portion of the people, to a corporation, or to a colony or dependency, assuring them certain rights, liberties or powers."[16] Thus charters should be understood as a grant of power from the state as the sovereign. According to Connecticut General Statutes 7-188-191, a proposal for charter adoption is initiated by a two-thirds vote of the board of selectman or by petition of 10 percent of the electors of the town. Within thirty days, a charter adoption commission must be appointed by the selectmen. It may number between five and fifteen, no more than one-third of the members may hold any other town office and not more than a bare majority can be of the same political party. Here is where the significant work begins. The commission then must hold at least two public hearings within sixteen months and submit a report to the appointing authority. The appointing authority must hold a public hearing within forty-five days of receiving the report and it may hold more hearings if it wishes. It has fifteen days after the final hearing to recommend any changes. The commission has thirty days to accept or reject any proposed changes. After the commission has accepted or rejected any changes, the appointing authority, within fifteen days, can by majority vote, (1 approve the charter or amendments and revision in total, (2 approve charter or amendments or revisions in part, (3 reject the charter or amendments and revisions in total or in part; the amendments so rejected cannot be acted on for one year. If a petition for a referendum vote for a charter is signed by 10 percent of the electorate and filed within forty-five days after the rejection, then the submission of the charter to the referendum becomes mandatory. The approved charter must be published within thirty days in a local newspaper. Within fifteen days of approval, the town clerk files three certified copies of the charter with the secretary of the state.

Form of Local Government

Form of local government refers to the nature of the relationship between the executive and legislative functions of government at the local level.[17] When an examination of local forms of government in Connecticut is undertaken, it is exactly this relationship, and not necessarily the titles of the actors or institutions being reviewed that is critical when determining their form. There are mayors that are largely ceremonial in function and have very little power. There are also mayors that also hold office where a city manager is the chief executive authority. There are first selectmen that work at their jobs full-time and have considerable authority. There are municipal legislative institutions called Boards of Aldermen, Town Councils and even one called a Board of Directors, yet they all serve primarily the same legislative function. What follows is a brief review of some of these major forms.

TABLE 7.2 Town Population and Form of Government in 2000

	Less than 2,000	2,000-5,000	5,001-10,000	10,001-20,000	20,001-50,000	Greater than 50,000
Selectman-Town Meeting	11	31	31	24	7	2
Council-Manager	0	0	1	12	15	4
Mayor-Council	0	0	2	9	9	11

Based upon U.S. Census, 2000. *Geographic Comparison Table, Connecticut Place and County Subdivision. and Local Government in Connecticut,* 2nd Edition by Frank Connolly, 2002.

What the above table suggests is that in Connecticut, most towns under 20,000 in population are governed under the selectman-town meeting form of government. Those municipalities having a population of over 10,000 are well represented by Mayor Council and Council Manager forms. The largest cities in Connecticut seem to follow the Mayor Council form more than the other two forms.[18]

Selectman-Town Meeting

Provided by the state statutes for use by all towns and cities in Connecticut is the Selectman-Town meeting form of government. It is the traditional form of local government in Connecticut. There are currently 106 municipalities with this form.[19] Early selectmen in Connecticut were called, "Townsmen" and appear in Hartford as early as 1639. The term also appears in the first Code of Laws in Connecticut in 1650. From these early times, selectmen had the power as the general superintendent and executive agent of town affairs.[20] Yet, as Bushman indicates, in the local town in 17th century Connecticut, "selectman were not to govern the people against their will, but on the contrary, to obey when the people spoke."[21]

Figure 7.2. Selectmen-Town Meeting Form of Government

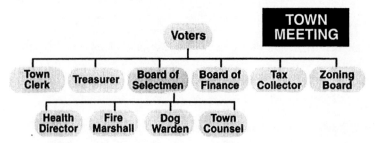

Selectmen must be electors of the town in which they reside. The selectmen hold their office as a board which is elected every two years. At different times in Connecticut's history, varying from town to town, there may have been as many as seven selectmen. By 1915, towns under 10,000 in population could elect no more than three to the board.[22] In a three-member board of selectmen, the first selectman candidates run in the election for the office of first selectman.

Within the board of selectmen, there is one individual who acts as first selectman. This is the person who serves as the day to day administrator of board activities for the town government. According to Section 7-12a of the Connecticut General Statutes, unless otherwise provided by law, the first selectman is the chief executive of the town, and serves as a non-voting member of all town boards and commissions. In many instances, this person serves on a full-time basis and receives a salary depending on the size of the municipality and how much administrative authority she or he may have. For example, there are some first selectmen in fairly large towns of over 40,000 in population which have adopted a charter, but have retained the position and title of first selectman. In the southwestern town of Greenwich, for example, in FY98-99, this full-time position received a salary of $83,000. By contrast, in northeastern Pomfret, a town under 5,000 in population, the position of first selectman received in the same year a salary of only $26,274.[23] Often the first selectman serves as road superintendent, welfare director, and coordinator of all the administrative offices.[24] Candidates for first selectman enjoy an interesting electoral benefit. According to Connecticut General Statute 9-187, when a person runs for the office of first selectman, and if she or he loses that election but receives more votes than a person running for the board of selectman, the losing candidate for first selectman can become a winning candidate for the board of selectman.

Coupled with the concept of the Board of Selectmen is the town meeting. Perhaps no other image brings the essence of grassroots democracy to mind as does the New England town meeting. Here, people of the town can come together face to face and deliberate and ultimately decide on the direction that town policy will take. Section 7-1 of the Connecticut General Statutes requires that, except as otherwise provided by law, there shall be in each town an annual town meeting to transact town business. Special town meetings can be called by the board of selectmen when they deem it necessary. Before the town meeting gets underway, the town clerk must "warn" or give prior notice of at least five days before the meeting. This is given by placing on a signpost near the office of the town clerk and by publishing a notice in a locally circulated newspaper. The warning must specify what business is to be conducted and any business not listed on the warning can not legally be considered (CGS 7-3). A moderator is chosen to run the meeting. The town clerk serves as clerk of the meeting and records all votes taken (CGS 7-23). As the legislative body of the town, the town meeting also acts upon the town budget at a special meeting designated as the annual budget meeting (CGS 7-388).

Anyone who is an elector of the town attaining the age of eighteen years and any person aged eighteen years who owns real estate listed on the town's grand list which is valued at $1,000 or more may vote at the town meeting (CGS 7-6).

The selectman-town meeting form of government is generally the form used by most municipalities with populations under 10,000.[25] Most of the towns governed under the selectman/town meeting form of government also have a board of finance which is provided for by Connecticut General Statute 7-340. This board has six members elected every two years. It is charged with requesting and receiving budget estimates from town agencies, evaluating agency requests, compiling the requests and presenting the budget to the town at the budget town meeting. The board of finance may reduce the budget approved by the board of education even though it develops and approves its own budget. While town and school budget are developed separately, together, as a whole, they comprise the town budget and are to be considered together for approval. Ultimately, the town meeting is the authority that passes the budget. The general government budget and the school budget should be voted on together. This was confirmed by the case, *Board of Education of Naugatuck v. Town and Borough of Naugatuck*.[26] If the budget does not pass, a new meeting of the people or a referendum if the people decide to vote by referendum, must be called where the budget must again be reconsidered. The town meeting may not appropriate more funds than recommended by the town meeting. It may also approve additional appropriations when requested (CGS 7-344).

In the smaller selectman-town meeting towns, it is still possible to have the electorate participate in a town meeting setting. In these towns, there is a great deal of participation on numerous elective boards and commissions required. There are boards of education, planning and zoning boards, boards of finance, boards of assessment appeals, library boards and inland/wetlands commissions. There are separately elected tax collectors, tax assessors, town clerks, and constables. This process usually ensures that issues are discussed thoroughly and decided upon by any who wish to participate. Numerous boards and commissions promote the concept of democratic checks and balances. In the ideal sense, this practice promotes our best desire for democracy: the ability of anyone who wishes to become involved, with no one person attaining too much power. On the other hand, critics have said that with such an extensive array of elective boards and commissions, the long election ballots are confusing and the wheels of government turn very slowly. Town meetings may not attract the number of people that would truly be reflective of the greater population and by their nature, are not always able to quickly respond to situations requiring expediency and executive leadership.

Six Connecticut towns have the selectman form of government but have modified it by instituting, through special acts, a Representative Town Meeting (RTM). Members of the RTMs are elected every two years and are chosen from districts based upon the population of the district. The RTM in effect acts as the people's representatives. The RTM exercises all of the powers of the town meeting, but its actions are usually subject to petition for referendum.[27] RTMs include Branford, Darien, Fairfield, Greenwich, Waterford and Groton.

Mayor-Council

Mayor-council forms of government in Connecticut are granted by charters. This form is distinguished by a single, chief elected official who has the title of mayor and an elected, unicameral representative body called the town or city council which is often elected by wards or districts. There are 31 mayor-council municipalities in Connecticut.[28]

Figure 7.3 Mayor-Council form (weak)

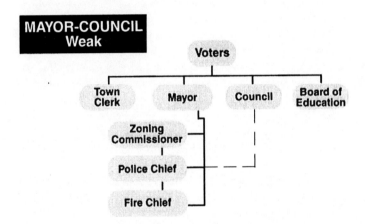

Figure 7.4 Mayor/Council form (strong)

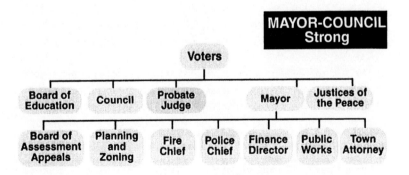

The mayor is the chief executive officer and usually works full-time as the chief administrator of the town or city. Mayors may be considered "weak" or "strong," depending on the council's power. Weak mayors usually lack the independent authority to make appointments and must rely on approval from their councils. The council serves as the legislative body of the local government. The council may be composed of anywhere from six to forty members and the number can vary even among the largest cities. For example, Stamford has a forty-member council. Waterbury has a fifteen-member council and Hartford has a nine-member council. Councils can be called town or city councils, boards of alderman or common councils. They are generally elected for two-year terms by districts but sometimes they are elected at-large, representing the entire municipality. For example, in the City of Hartford, the city council has the power to adopt ordinances regarding the safety and welfare of their towns; it has the power to adopt resolutions which can change or create a policy, or acknowledge people and events; it can also review zoning laws and revise inland/wetland maps.[29] In Connecticut, some council members are paid for their service and some are not. Council members in Hartford receive $15,000; Bridgeport council members receive no pay.

Weak mayors usually lack the independent authority to appoint department heads. They may not make these high level hiring decisions without the consent of the council, which may reflect district and not town wide interests.[30] Weak mayors may also lack the ability to develop budgetary policy for their city or town having a board of finance that assumes this responsibility. Other boards and commissions that are independently elected have the effect of further decentralizing policy decisions, contributing to the lack of executive leadership. An example might include Milford, where the mayor prepares the town budget for submission to the board of finance. After holding its budget hearings, the board of finance, not the mayor, makes its budget recommendations to the town's board of aldermen.[31]

In the 1950's, in Hartford, the mayor was actually the councilman who received the most votes. A charter change in the 1960s made the office of mayor a separately elected office.[32] The mayor of Hartford had to work with the city manager who technically was the chief administrator.

"Strong" mayors, on the other hand, reflect a more centralized approach to local government in Connecticut. Found frequently in larger cities, the leadership role of the mayor as chief administrator is emphasized. As mayor, she or he is directly responsible to the voters and the mayor has authority to appoint the department heads who will work within the mayor's administration to execute her or his agenda. In general, there may be fewer independently elected officials. Councils under the strong mayor form may have some powers of appointment for certain boards and commissions, but it is clearly the mayor who exercises leadership.[33] Examples include: Hamden, East Haven, Vernon, Stamford, New Haven, and Waterbury. While strong mayors may enjoy a formal structure that promotes executive leadership, the formal structure is rarely sufficient to move the mayor's agenda. Often a mayor must rely on personal powers to achieve the policy ends they desire. In his seminal book on group democracy, *Who Governs?*, Robert Dahl, in 1961, wrote about the New Haven mayor of that era. According to Dahl, "He rarely commanded. He negotiated, cajoled, exhorted, beguiled, charmed, pressed, appealed, reasoned, promised, insisted, demanded, even threatened, but he most needed support and acquiescence from other leaders who simply could not be commanded. Because the mayor could not command, he had to bargain."[34]

The strong mayor city of Stamford first elected Dannel P. Malloy in 1995. Under a charter revision which gave the mayor a four-year term of office, he was re-elected in 1997. Included among his accomplishments are: school construction, establishment of a youth services bureau, the sale of city properties, and the establishment of neighborhood police substations. According to Malloy, "Stamford's strong mayor form of government allows its leader to leverage the responsibilities of the position and the power of the bully pulpit to innovate, restructure, modernize and strengthen our city. Combined with leadership, a capable and committed work force and a shared vision for change, this system is a formula for success."[35]

Council-Manager

Considered as a product of government reform, the basic idea behind the council-manager form of government is to remove partisan politics from the efficient administration of local government. All council-manager forms of government are also granted by charter. There are thirty-two council-manager forms in Connecticut.[36] Many council manager forms were granted through special acts of the General Assembly and adopted by referendum prior to the home rule law. West Hartford was the first town in Connecticut to have the council-manager form of government. It was granted a charter through a special act of the legislature in 1920.[37] Other examples include: Coventry, Killingly, New London, Mansfield, Manchester, Hartford, and Wethersfield.

Figure 7.5   Council-Manager Form

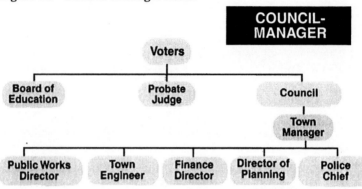

Under this form, the legislative body is the town or city council. It is a powerful, but usually smaller council that controls the chief executive, which is the town or city manager. The town or city manager is a professional, specifically trained manager who usually has an earned master's degree in public administration. Many town and city managers are active in an organization called the International City/County Management Association (ICMA) which provides professional development and training throughout their careers. This manager is appointed by the town council and is subject to removal by the town council at any time.

The manager has the authority to appoint and remove the city's department heads as chief executive. The town manager also is directly responsible for the preparation of the town's annual budget. The town manager must be free to exercise their managerial authority. If a town's boards and commission create undo restraints on the manager's authority, executive leadership can become fragmented.[38] In an interview with *The Hartford Courant*, former City Manager of Hartford Gene Shipman has said, "The council manager form of government is the best that this country has to offer in terms of ensuring that the government is well managed and fiscally healthy and has an effective and efficient service delivery system. The checks and balances fall out the window when you go to a strong mayor form of government."[39]

While the intent of the council-manager form is to bring non-partisan professionalism to local government, some have criticized this form as being undemocratic. After all, goes the argument, the town manager need not come from the town or city at all. They may not know or appreciate the culture of a specific municipality. How can they reflect the will of the people? The answer to this is that reflecting the will of the people is left up to the council, who are elected by the people and ultimately hold the key to the manager's position.

Key Municipal Officials

No matter what form of government a town or city has, there are several key general government offices besides the mayor, first selectman or town manager that are present under most forms. These specialized offices provide a range of necessary and essential governmental services for their municipalities. What follows is a summary of the most commonly found general government officials found in Connecticut local government.

Town Clerk

In Connecticut, the office of the town or city clerk is the primary source for municipal records. These extensive records include land records, marriage records, birth records, hunting and fishing licenses, dog licenses and voter registration records. These records must be kept in fire proof vaults for safe-keeping. The clerk's office is the repository for the schedule and minutes of meetings for town boards and commissions. The clerk is also the official keeper of the town seal. In towns having the selectman-town meeting form of government, the town clerk serves as the clerk of the town meeting and records all votes and actions taken. Where the council serves as the legislative body, the clerk serves as clerk of the council. As the chief local election official, it is the town clerk who officially swears in newly elected members to their boards and commissions.

Tax Assessor

In Connecticut, property taxes are the prime sources of local government revenue. The assessment and collection of property taxes are determined by state law but administered separately by local officials. The property tax is an ad valorem tax, that is, a tax based upon the value of taxable real or personal property such as real estate, improvements on land, and certain kinds of equipment and motor vehicles. It is the municipal assessor that places the value on this real and personal property. The assessor conducts her or his business by first discovering the property, listing it and pricing it. By state law, a complete revaluation of all taxable property within the municipality must be completed at least every four years. The assessor may use any of three approaches to determine value of real property. The first of these three approaches is called the market or sales approach. Here, an analysis of the sales of comparable properties is undertaken. A property is reviewed in comparison with other similar properties within the same period of time. By looking at the sale prices of comparable properties, a value is derived for the property in question.

The second approach used in property valuation is called the cost approach. This approach values a property by estimating what the replacement or reproduction costs of a structure might be, factoring in an estimate of accrued depreciation. The third approach used by assessors to value property is the income approach. Here, the property is valued according to the amount of income it may be able to produce. By state law, assessors in Connecticut place the value of a property at 70 percent of its fair market value. This brings more uniformity to the valuation process across the state.

Once the process of discovery, listing and pricing is completed, the assessor is responsible for compiling an official listing of all taxable property within the municipality. This listing is called the Grand List. It represents the assessed value of all taxable real and personal property as well as tax-exempt property. By statute, the date of this assessment is placed on October 1 of every year. The net Grand List, is the total assessed value after exemptions are deducted. This becomes the tax base for the municipality. Over time, economic conditions and thus property values can change and a considerable variance in the value of real estate in the same town may occur. Every four years, according to state law, all real property within a town or city must undergo a process of revaluation. In this process, all taxable property is reappraised in an effort to more accurately reflect the fair market value of all real property and ensure an equitable distribution of the tax burden to property owners within the town.

Tax Collector

When the municipality adopts its budget each year, the town meeting or city council in effect decides how much money in taxes must be raised to cover the expenses of government. The rate of tax to be applied is determined by dividing the amount of tax money needed by the taxable Grand List. This basic equation yields a mill rate or tax rate that is expressed in mills or tenths of one cent. For example, a derived mill rate of .0250 or 25 mills means that for every $1,000 of assessed value of a property, the tax would be $25.

By Connecticut General Statute, 12-130, the tax collection process begins when appropriate town public officials such as the first selectman makes out and signs rate bills which indicate how much each individual property owner must pay according to the assessment list. These rate bills are given to the tax collector along with a warrant issued by a judge of the Superior Court or a justice of the peace directing the tax collector to collect the taxes and, if necessary, to impose any penalties required. The tax collector must mail or hand deliver to each individual a bill for the amount of taxes due. According to Connecticut General Statute 12-145, failure to receive a tax bill does not invalidate the tax or interest. The tax collector turns over the monies collected to the Town Treasurer. The tax collector also makes any necessary corrections, abatements or refunds.

Board of Finance

The board of finance is the board in many Connecticut towns that is charged with overseeing the town's financial administration and maintaining a sound fiscal policy. Within this capacity, the board of finance also administers the municipal budgetary process in preparing and reviewing the annual town budget. It is generally composed of six members. Three alternate members may be appointed by town ordinance. Under the state statutes, the board is responsible for preparing the town budget, setting the mill rate, approving transfers of monies between appropriations and approving budget deficiencies, setting up a system of keeping financial records, providing for an annual audit of town accounts and publishing the annual town report.[40]

In larger towns, there may be a specialized finance department which takes the place of the board in the fiscal administration of the town.

This department is generally responsible for keeping the town's financial accounts and funds in order, making appropriate investments of town funds and administering the town payroll.

Streets and Highways Superintendent

The maintenance of a town's or city's infrastructure is a necessary task to perform and is very important to a community's quality of life. The main job of this individual is to administer and oversee the cleaning, maintenance and repair of all public streets within the town. This usually includes snow removal, sanding and salting in the winter, removal of downed trees and other hazards and the cleaning and maintenance of catch basins and drains. In some towns, the highway department also includes leaf pick-up, household trash pick-up, and bulky waste disposal. Other duties may include sidewalk installation, erecting traffic signs, mowing public grass areas and cemetery maintenance.

Planning Commission

Towns in Connecticut are required to prepare a town plan of development to guide the best use of town land for future development. This plan shows the most desirable use of land for residential, recreational, commercial and industrial use. The planning commission's task is to develop this plan and amend or revise it as necessary. It has authority for approving the location of roads, subdivisions, public buildings and utilities. Some municipalities combine the planning function with zoning. Zoning deals with the locations within a town of where particular types of building and land use can occur. A zoning enforcement officer usually has the task of making sure that town residents comply with town zoning regulations.

Public Safety

Many Connecticut municipalities have their own professionally trained police, fire and emergency medical services. Public safety may be provided by large, multi-unit departments that might include a Special Weapons and Tactics team (SWAT) within the larger cities to relatively small departments with limited resources in the smaller towns. In some of the smaller towns, instead of there being a municipal police force, there may be a resident state trooper. This is a State Police Officer who has complete law enforcement authority within a municipality. Other small towns do not even have a resident state trooper, but rely on a state trooper dispatched from one of twelve regional state police barracks. In many of the smaller towns, fire and emergency medical services are provided by volunteers who receive extensive professional training and state certification in their fields.

Other municipal officials typically found within town government carry out their responsibilities in public health, social services, parks and recreation, wetlands protection, economic development, and building maintenance.

Special Districts

These are areas in which special services to citizens are provided. They are established by special acts of the legislature or through a process provided by Chapter 105 of the state statutes. Special districts, like boroughs, provide particular services for an area including fire protection, street lighting, sewer and flood, and erosion control. There may be a special property tax levy made for the provision of these districts within the town or city. In 1988, the Connecticut Advisory Commission on Intergovernmental Relations concluded that there were 258 special districts within the state; 158 of these were created under procedures laid out within state statutes and 100 by special acts of the legislature. Special districts independently manage their own finances and may issue bonds for any public works project within their scope of authority. Neither the state or the town in which they are located play a role in governing a special district. Voters select the officers of the district who are responsible for conducting district business.[41]

Local Education in Connecticut

In 1644, the General Court required settlements of fifty or more families to appoint a school master, whose salary was to be paid by children's parents, their masters, or by the inhabitants of the town in general. When the population reached 100 families, the town was ordered to set up a grammar school to prepare its youth for entrance into the university.[42]

While it was generally a local responsibility to control elementary and secondary schools, in 1838, a State Board of Commissioners for Education was established to supervise the schools. In 1865, a State Board of Education replaced the Board of Commissioners. This board has nine members appointed by the governor and its job is to enforce state educational policies. As was seen earlier, Article Eighth of the Connecticut Constitution states that, "There shall always be free public elementary and secondary schools in the state. The General Assembly shall implement this principle by appropriate legislation."[43]

The *Horton vs. Meskill* case,[44] decided in 1977, found unacceptable disparities among individual school district spending due to reliance on real estate taxes for education purposes. Through a formula, enacted by the state legislature, the state has mandated a minimum expenditure requirement (MER) which must be spent for each student in each municipality. Under the MER, some expenditures, for example, transportation for students, adult education and special education, do not count towards the minimum spending. Connecticut towns and cities have discretion on what to spend their education money on within the guidelines, as long as they do not go below the minimum. The district must report its expenditures to the state every year, and if the district has gone below the MER, the State Board of Education may withhold grant funds, up to two times the amount of the deficiency, from the district in the following year.[45]

While the State's MER mandates what municipalities must spend on local education, Education Cost Sharing or ECS grants referred to in Connecticut General Statutes 10-262, are the primary vehicle for the state to assist local elementary and secondary schools. It is generally the largest state grant to Connecticut municipalities. Beginning in 1988, the ECS grants were formulated as a way that local education spending could achieve equalization across municipalities. The formula for these grants takes into account property wealth, income, number of students, student performance, student poverty and a foundation cost figure. Given a certain uniform level of property wealth, every town and city in Connecticut could spend a minimum amount of money for the education of its children. When a town falls short of that minimum level of wealth, the state makes a grant to make up the difference. Since 1995, the amount that a town's ECS grant may grow has been capped. The early goal of this initiative was for both the state and municipalities to share the expenses for education equally by each funding education by 50 percent. In practice, the state has consistently spent below the 50 percent level, hovering in the range of 39-42 percent over the last several years and increasing the burden for education on the towns.[46] In the 2000-01 state budget, primary and secondary education accounted for almost 16.8 percent of state spending, while education took up about 57 percent of municipal budgets during the same time period.[47]

Students with emotional, physical or mental disabilities also deserve a public education to prepare them under the best possible means for a meaningful and productive future. These children are entitled to a "free appropriate public education." Under the federal, Individuals with Disabilities Act (IDEA) students with these disabilities in need of specially designed instruction at the district level, come under the heading of special education.[48] School districts are required by law to educate these students and over time, these special education costs have become one of the most critical issues that local boards have been required to address. Special instruction, curriculum, and facilities required for individual children, all serve to increase costs in this area. The state provides school districts with Excess Cost Grants, which help to reimburse municipalities a portion of special education costs once these costs have passed a specific threshold. The expense threshold for local districts, provided by Connecticut General Statute 10-76g(b), is five times the average cost of regular education per student.[49] Gifted and talented children in Connecticut also come under the special education law, but school districts are not required to provide this group of students with special education.[50]

Boards of Education

Connecticut General Statute 10-220 provides that towns, through their boards of education, shall maintain good public elementary and secondary schools and implement the educational interests of the state and provide educational activities that will best serve the interest of the school district. This includes providing adequate instructional resources such as books, facilities and staff, an equitable distribution of resources among district schools and a safe school setting. The board, therefore, is the chief policy-making body for educational issues within the school district. Thomas Mooney has said that this requirement places a dual role on local school boards. From the municipal perspective, school boards are composed of locally elected citizens serving their community. From the point of view of the state, state law requires that they serve as state agents in implementing the educational interests of the state.[51]

Most boards of education are composed of seven to nine members. There are 166 public school districts in Connecticut, containing 655 elementary schools, 169 middle schools, 163 high schools and seventy-one non-graded Pre-K schools. As Table 7.3 demonstrates, public school enrollment in general has seen a significant increase during the 1990s.[52]

Table 7.3 Public School Enrollment 1992-1993 and 1999-2000

	1992-93	1999-00	% Increase
Non-graded, Pre-K	14,834	14,131	(5)%
Elementary-Junior High	346,048	390,657	13%
High School	128,767	150,070	17%

Source: Connecticut State Department of Education, *Profiles of Our Schools: The Condition of Education in Connecticut 1999-2000*, (2001)

A major task of the board is to review the education budget. Education is often the largest component of any municipal budget in Connecticut, in most cases accounting for over 50 percent of the municipal budget. Boards of education in Connecticut prepare their own annual budgets, but are subject to review and modification by municipal boards of finance or the authority making appropriations for the school district such as the town council. In towns under the selectman-town meeting form, the town meeting may vote to reduce the board of education's budget as well as the town budget. Typically, the school board will hire and evaluate the school superintendent, who serves as the chief administrative officer of the school district. The superintendent is a professional with a special advanced degree and certification in education administration. Boards must also oversee the maintenance of school facilities, negotiate labor contracts for both professional and support staff and determine policy for school functions and activities.

Sometimes, it may be in the interest of two or more boards to share their resources. Regional boards are cooperative entities made up of two or more towns to serve the educational needs of their communities on a joint basis and once created, have the same powers and authorities as local boards.

Boroughs

There are eight boroughs within Connecticut. They operate as separate units of government within towns. They all were chartered through special acts of the General Assembly to take care of specific local needs of densely populated areas of rural towns. The purpose of a borough, typically, is to oversee such government functions as street maintenance, police and fire protection and health and sanitation services. The borough levies property taxes to provide the needed services. In Connecticut the boroughs are: Danielson (in the town of Killingly), Fenwick (in the town of Old Saybrook), the Woodmont Association (within the town of Milford), Bantam and Litchfield (in Litchfield), Jewett City (in Griswold), Newtown (in Newtown) and Stonington (in Stonington). The chief elected official in a borough is called the warden and members of its legislative body are called the burgesses.[53]

The Local Budget Process in Connecticut

·   The fiscal year in Connecticut is a uniform twelve-month period running from July 1 to June 30, and in which local governments operate and spend the money appropriated to them. In Connecticut, unlike many states, local government operations are mostly funded primarily by the local property tax. In 1996, for example, the Connecticut Policy and Economic Council reported that local property taxes accounted for almost 65 percent of local government revenues. About 26 percent of local revenues came from state grants.[54] This left about 10 percent coming from local permits, fees and other sources.

A review of the budget of any town or city reveals what was considered most important at the time of its adoption. A town budget can be seen as the end product of the political process reflecting the needs and wants of specific constituencies within the town. There are many interests that may have an influence on the budget. There may be neighborhood groups wanting certain improvements; seniors looking for additional programs; taxpayers associations looking to keep taxes low; and the press looking to scrutinize government deficiencies in delivering public services. Are there increasing numbers of new families moving into town? Look for more expenditures within the school budget and perhaps the recreation department. Has there been more residential development? Look for increases in the road maintenance or sanitation budget.

Municipal budgets usually have four phases; preparation, approval, execution and audit. In the preparation phase, local government agencies begin to plan and prepare their budget requests usually based upon guidelines provided by the chief executive official.

The process of preparation usually begins at the end of the calendar year in early December. By January, budget submissions are beginning the review process. Agencies present and defend their budgets to the chief executive. By March, a detailed analysis of expected revenues and expenditures is undertaken. By April, public hearings on the budget are conducted to get community input. Changes and modifications may occur. After hearings are completed by May, the reviewed budgets are presented to the town meeting, town or city council or to referendum for voting by the town. The town and board of education budgets are passed separately. If one of them fails, both must come back again for another vote before the town has a budget. Once the budget is approved by the legislative body or by town vote, the budget becomes a legally binding document. The passage of the budget allows the appropriate governing body to set the mill rate which will determine the local taxes to be collected. The budget is now ready for execution. It is the plan of how revenues will be collected and money will be spent by the agencies of the municipality. An independent auditor is hired by the municipality to ensure that execution of the budget is in compliance with how the budget was legally adopted.

No County Government

There is an almost unique element about sub-state government in Connecticut. There is no county government. Only one other state in the United States, Rhode Island, does not have county government. Yet, at one time, it did exist in Connecticut. Rosaline Levinson has written that Connecticut was the second state in the nation to establish county government and was the first state in the Union to abolish it in 1960.[55] Connecticut continues to have geographic areas designated as counties: Hartford, New Haven, Fairfield, New London, Middlesex, Tolland and Windham. These are used chiefly for statistics keeping purposes and to designate different geographical parts of the state.

When Connecticut had a viable county government, it had mainly the following functions: administration of the county jails, courthouse maintenance, adjustment of road disputes, administration of certain kinds of trust funds, lending agricultural assistance, assisting the funding of public hospitals, caring for neglected children, and providing fire fighting assistance. The administration of the counties was accomplished through a three-member board of commissioners which, unlike most other states, were appointed by the General Assembly. Each county also had an elected High Sheriff, whose chief functions were to manage the county jail, law enforcement, courthouse functions and serving civil process.[56]

Over time, functions traditionally given to county government in Connecticut were largely taken over by state government. The formation of the state highway department in 1895 and the creation of the state police in 1903 took those responsibilities away from the county government. State public assistance took over for county welfare programs, like Widow's Aid. By the middle of the 20th century, the conditions of the county jail systems began to drastically disintegrate, and the treatment of prisoners was considered below standard.[57] Jail house disorders and disturbances were becoming a too common experience for the county jail system.[58] Also at this time there emerged harsh criticism of the treatment of children living at various county homes.[59] County government in Connecticut, it seems, had been struggling for a long time.

The county governments were heavily criticized by Democrats within the state and Republicans, while not out rightly favoring abolishment, sought to reform and improve them. Abraham Ribicoff, in his quest for the governor's office, openly campaigned against them. The 1958 state elections saw the Democrats winning a large victory which gave them considerable strength in the General Assembly. This electoral victory enabled the Democrats to push through the General Assembly their bill for eventual county abolition.[60] As a result, the state of Connecticut assumed, for the most part, the functions and responsibilities formerly carried out by the counties.

The county sheriffs, due to their Constitutional status, remained the last vestige of county governmental office until they too were eliminated in a vote for a constitutional amendment on November 7, 2000. In that ballot, the sheriffs went down in defeat, loosing by a vote of 585,155 to abolish and 307,275 to retain the office.[61]

Regionalism

In the absence of county government, and with a sizable number of special districts, school districts, and local governments among the 169 towns and cities, it would not be too difficult to imagine that there would be at least some duplication of effort in municipal affairs. Realizing this inevitability, towns and cities do work together in certain areas where it makes sense to do so. Cooperation between municipalities may come in the form of a formal agreement authorized by state statute or may be completely voluntary. The Connecticut Advisory Commission on Intergovernmental Relations has reported that there are approximately thirty-seven types of cooperative or regional organizations authorized by state or federal law.[62] These generally take the the following forms:

1. Cooperative general government organizations specifically required or authorized by state or federal law.
2. Inter-district and regional education programs organized under specific legislation.
3. More informal general government agreements which are the products of inter-municipal contracts or local agreements.
4. Other kinds of inter-district educational programs organized locally to provide needed services.
5. Inter-district agreements formed among previously constituted regional groups.[63] For example, there are sixteen regional health districts within the state. Under the Federal Aid Highway Act of 1973, to provide transportation policy direction, the state has nine Metropolitan Planning Organizations (MPOs). Under Connecticut General Statutes 7-273aa to 7-273oo, there are six municipal Resource Recovery Authorities for solid waste processing. There are also twelve regional transit districts formed for the purpose of developing and improving mass transportation. Under Connecticut General Statute 10-66a to 10-66n there are six Regional Educational Service Centers which are tasked with providing cooperative educational programs and services to member municipalities. Under Connecticut General Statute 10-39-63t, regional school districts may be set up, by a referendum vote of each participating community, to provide education services to a multi-district area. There are seventeen regional school districts in Connecticut.

Under Connecticut General Statutes 4-124c-4-124h, regional planning may take the form of Regional Planning Agencies (RPAs), Regional Councils of Elected Officials (CEOs) and Regional Councils of Governments (COGs). The state is divided into fifteen planning regions. Under Connecticut General Statutes 8-31a to 8-37b, regional planning agencies (RPAs) are created by ordinance by two or more towns within a region which agree to do so. Each member town can send two representatives, and an additional representative at the rate of one for each 50,000 of population, or fraction thereof, over a base population of 25,000. Representatives are chosen by local ordinance and are not generally elected officials. CEOs are formed when the legislative bodies of at least two of the municipalities within the planning region agree through ordinances to do so. The towns' chief elected officials represent the towns at the council with one vote each. Councils of governments are formed when at least 60 percent of the municipalities within a region approve ordinances to that effect. Each town sends its chief elected official to represent it at the Council of Government. These bodies represent the highest form of regional planning in Connecticut. Formation of a COG supercedes any existing Regional Planning Agency or Council of Elected Officials.[64]

Some good examples of the kinds of cooperative efforts that municipalities can participate in can be found in the Capital Region Council of Governments, which is composed of twenty-nine towns and cities in the Greater Hartford area. The Capitol Region Jobs Access Program provides transportation access to jobs for people who depend on public transportation to get to their jobs. The Capitol Region Public Safety Council supported the development of a Mobil Data Communication System for police departments within the region. It provides instant police access to local, state and federal criminal information files.[65]

State Representative Jefferson Davis believes that one of Connecticut's greatest challenges is to address the economic segregation of its citizens. This challenge is greatest in Connecticut's large cities which have suffered from poverty, crime, racial segregation, poor education and loss of population. He points out the need for Connecticut to be considered as a group of regional economies which transcend local political boundaries if meaningful and significant economic development is to take place. One area of focus is on the development of metropolitan areas where cities and towns work together for mutual benefit on such areas as property tax reform, block grants to regional councils of governments, rental and down payment on new home assistance and building business clusters to promote industrial growth.[66] Others are not so convinced about the prospects of regionalism in Connecticut. According to Leigh Standish, under regionalism, the burden of addressing the financial and social problems of Connecticut's cities would unfairly shift to nearby suburbs. He argues that the regional governing bodies, as more remote than local governments, would not be able to adequately respond to local concerns.[67]

State Senator Judith Freedman, while supporting mutually beneficial agreements between towns freely arrived at, has said, "Most municipal leaders, particularly those in the smaller towns, do not need nor want the state interfering in any way to force communities into formal regional arrangements."[68]

Connecticut is a small state that has experienced through its history a unique relationship between the dual traditions of state authority and local identity. Before the apportionment cases of the 1960s, it was the individual towns and cities that sent their representatives to Hartford under a scheme of government that practically nullified any differences that size or location could make. By the late 1950s, Connecticut citizens realized that county government could not provide any services that the state could not provide better. Local government, for some, will always be seen as the mere creature of state policy. Yet, local government is closest to the people and seems to hold much promise for creatively tackling the challenges for government that lie ahead.

Chapter 8

Connecticut's State of Democracy

*We cannot afford the luxury of frustration or inaction. Democracy requires
our constant engagement, and it demands persistence from us.*

Leslie Brett,
Executive Director of the
Connecticut Permanent Commission
on the Status of Women.[1]

This review of Connecticut's state and local governments demonstrates that there are governmental institutions, structures, and political processes and practices within the state that would fulfill most of our expectations for what might normally be required for a democracy. But to what extent are those expectations fulfilled? Connecticut has a constitution which provides the basic governmental framework and which spells out the rights of state citizens, there is a separation of powers between governmental institutions which provide checks and balances, there are legal mechanisms and laws in place to ensure individual and equal political representation to the greatest extent possible at the state and local levels of government. Yet formal structures that may provide democratic representation have never been adequate to ensure that democracy is practiced. To offer a judgment on how well democracy is practiced in any society is a task that requires a long term and ongoing examination conducted within a free and open debate. This last chapter will focus on some specific efforts that have been made to analyze the state of democracy in Connecticut.

State Benchmarks for Democracy

In 1996, Connecticut Secretary of the State Miles Rapoport, commissioned a groundbreaking study for the purpose of assessing the state of democracy in Connecticut. The problems and issues of assessing and measuring democracy in Connecticut were given considerable and careful thought by an advisory board composed of many people from a variety of organizations and fields. This inaugural report established a set of five benchmarks through which could be viewed how the process of democracy was practiced in Connecticut. The benchmarks established were: Knowledge and Interest, Participation and Commitment; Social and Economic Equality and Opportunity; Tolerance and Diversity and Commonweal.[2] This report was followed up with a second effort in 1998. In 2000, a new Secretary of the State, Susan Bysiewicz published a third report, utilizing the same benchmarks but focusing on the youth of Connecticut.

The first report in 1996 stated that, "If this were a report card, the grade would fall somewhere between 'needs improvement' and 'satisfactory', with a number of comments in the margin highlighting examples of excellent effort."[3] Borrowing the definition used in *Webster's II New Riverside Dictionary*, the original report defined democracy as:

1. government exercised directly by the people of through elected representatives,

2. a political or social unit based on democratic rule,

3. rule by the majority and

4. principles of social equality and respect for the individual within a community.

According to the report, while Connecticut had made some excellent efforts in terms of extending democracy according to this type of definition, it was clear that more work remained to be done. Highlights from the three reports concerning the five benchmarks follow. They, as well as other selected sources, will help to illustrate the state of democracy in Connecticut.

Democracy requires an informed citizenry to work at its best. The benchmark of knowledge and interest attempted to address how Connecticut citizens become informed and learn about public issues within their state and communities and also about the availability of opportunities and resources to practice democracy. At a conference held in Connecticut as a follow-up to the *1996 Report*, then U.S. Senator Bill Bradley, as the keynote speaker, noted that dialogue was critical to the idea of a living democracy. Developing the skills of dialogue can help us to acquire knowledge, maintain interest and further democracy.[4] The role of the media cannot be understated as a main means of informing citizens. Under this benchmark, the 1996 report stated that Connecticut, at almost 80 percent, was among the leading states in the nation in the percentage of households that subscribe to cable TV. The state's largest newspaper, *The Hartford Courant*, in 1996 had a daily circulation of 208,446. The *Journal Register Company*, which publishes daily papers in New Britain, Bristol, Middletown and New Haven, had a combined daily circulation of 173,694. Yet these numbers reflected a general decline in newspaper circulation.[5] The *2000 Report* commented on the low level of political interest of many Connecticut citizens across generations. During the month of August, 1999, Quinnipiac College conducted a poll on political interest among Connecticut residents of various age groups. The poll reported that only 16 percent Generation X (18-35 year olds), had a high interest in politics. This compares with 25 percent of the Baby Boomers (ages 35-53) surveyed, and 40 percent of the Matures (ages 54+).[6]

There are organizations in Connecticut working hard to address these kinds of survey results. The League of Women Voters of Connecticut has been a key organization in the state for democratic education. The League promotes voter registration, sponsors candidate forums and publishes educational materials on state and local government processes. The Connecticut Consortium for Law and Citizenship Education, Inc. is an organization that teaches civic education to Connecticut's youth. It sponsors activities such as debates and mock trials and provides educational materials for civics.

The benchmark of participation and commitment sought to analyze how the people of Connecticut became involved in democratic practices.

Probably the most recognizable characteristic of democratic participation is voter registration and voter turnout. The *1996 Report* described Connecticut's efforts at registration and turnout as mediocre. With about 75 percent of Connecticut's eligible voters registered to vote, when compared to the other 49 states, the state was ranked in the middle. This represented a significant decline since the 1950s when it ranked in the top ten for voter registration.[7] After a sustained and creative effort by the Secretary of the State to improve voter registration, the *1998 Report* published that a record 85.6 percent of the estimated voting age population in Connecticut were registered to vote by the fall of 1996.[8] Yet high voter registration does not necessarily mean high voter turnout. The following table demonstrates that between 1990 and 2000 Connecticut has experienced a range of political participation as expressed by voter turnout, with a high in 1992 of almost 84 percent and a low in 1998 of just over 56 percent.[9]

Table 8.1 Election Day Registration and Turnout 1990-2000

Year	Number on Voting List	Number That Voted	% That Voted
2000	1,901,203	1,474,103	77.54
1998	1,806,750	1,022,453	56.59
1996	1,881,323	1,410,476	74.97
1994	1,791,685	1,166,162	65.09
1992	1,961,503	1,645,609	83.90
1990	1,700,871	1,159,361	68.16

Source: Secretary of the State, *Connecticut State Register and Manual*, 1990, 1992, 1994, 1996,1998, 2000.

Another measure of participation is public service. A 1996, University of Connecticut, Institute of Public Service survey sought to measure the amount of citizen participation of local public boards and commissions. With 156 of Connecticut's 169 municipalities responding, it was estimated that about 30,000 people serve on local boards and commissions or as local officers, including selectmen, library boards, planning and zoning, justices of the peace, constables and many others.[10]

Richard Porth, Executive Director of the Capital Region Council of Governments makes the case that, "Connecticut's historic roots in the town meeting form of government provide an excellent platform on which to rebuild civic participation."[11]

Connecticut is home to the Study Circles Resource Center, an organization founded by philanthropist Paul Aicher which has achieved national recognition for its efforts at developing and promoting community and civic dialogue on critical social issues. Study circles are small groups of people formed at the community level which engage in discussion around an issue through a structured process and which include reading materials focused on the issue from different perspectives. The intent is to realize that there may be several ways to approach an issue and to give each perspective a fair opportunity for expression. Meeting over several sessions, participants come to a better understanding of different points of view and begin a consensus building process. Often the study circles lead to action plans which have a direct impact on the community in which they were formed. Hundreds of Connecticut citizens have engaged in study circles formed around such issues as community citizenship, race relations, school readiness and quality of education.[12] Other hardworking grassroots organizations in Connecticut include Democracy Works, The Connecticut Citizen Action Group, Common Cause of Connecticut and the Federation of Connecticut Taxpayer Organizations.

Social and economic equality is thought to be an integral part of living within a democracy because without real equality, democratic participation loses its meaning. Leslie J. Brett, Executive Director of the Connecticut Permanent Commission on the Status of Women has said, "A democracy cannot fully function on behalf of all of its citizens if only some of its citizens share fully in the rewards and benefits that society provides."[13] The ability to work and earn a living is important for the practice of democracy. The *1996 Report* cited Connecticut losing 162,000 jobs between 1989-1995.[14] Yet the *Social State of Connecticut 2001 Report* found that in 1999 the unemployment rate in the state was 3.2 percent, the best since 1988.[15] The nature of Connecticut's workforce has continued to change. Manufacturing jobs continue to decline, while service sector jobs, which characteristically have lower wages, continue to grow.[16] While Connecticut's per capita personal income continued to be the highest in the nation, the *1998 Report* cites U.S. Census data which placed 10.7 percent of the state's population within the poverty level which at that time was $14,600 for a family of four.[17] The city that experienced the largest increase in its rate of poverty in the entire state between 1989 and 1999 was East Hartford.[18] In the state's most urban areas, there can be found the highest percentages of children living in poverty; 46 percent in Hartford, 33 percent in New Haven and 30 percent in Bridgeport.[19] The distance between the incomes of the highest and lowest counties in Connecticut in 1999, was the greatest recorded since 1970.[20]

This situation has given rise to the practice of talking about the "two states" of Connecticut—one rich and one poor. For example, in the period from the late 1980s to the late 1990s, the poorest 20 percent of Connecticut's residents saw a drop in their average annual income of

26 percent. For the same period, the average annual income for the state's wealthiest residents rose by 18 percent.[21] Of 169 towns and cities in Connecticut, the town with the highest median household income in 1999 was Weston with $120,272. This was five times higher than the town with the lowest median household income which was Hartford, with $23, 320 and two times higher than the statewide average of $55,173.22. Out of 1.3 million households in Connecticut, more than 55,000 make more than $200,000 annually. About 86,260 households earn less than $10,000 annually. About 186,550 receive some form of public assistance or non-cash benefits.[23] Statistics generated by the U.S. Census Bureau for the 2000 Census indicated that the capitol city of Hartford was the poorest town or city in Connecticut with 31 percent of its residents at or below the poverty line.[24] According to Rachel Ranis, a Quinnipiac University sociology professor, "We're a state of the very wealthy and the poorest poor-like a developing country. The gap is very frightening."[25]

The history of American democracy has been one of ever expanding political and civil rights for individuals of diverse cultures and races. The benchmark of Tolerance and Diversity sought to look at how the practice of democracy has been expanded amongst diverse individuals. While Connecticut remains predominantly white, it is growing in its diversity. The *1998 Report* states that since 1990, people of African-American descent have increased 6 percent, the Hispanic population has increased 19 percent and Asians have increased 40 percent. But Connecticut's population does not reflect the diversity of the nation as a whole.[26]

A report prepared by the Office of the Secretary of the State in March 2000, called *Gender and Racial Diversity on Connecticut State Appointive Bodies, 1999*, examined the diversity of the state's 203 state boards, commissions, committees and councils. There were a total of 1,997 appointed members serving on these various bodies. Of these, the report stated that 34.3 percent were women and 65.7 percent were men; 89.4 percent were white, 6.6 percent were black, 2.7 percent were Hispanic. This report concludes that women are under-represented and that diversity is not reflected as well as it could be on these bodies.[27]

The lack of toleration of differences, and how it sometimes becomes violent, continues to be a challenge requiring attention. Hate crime offences are crimes motivated by bias and bigotry in relation to race, religion, ethnicity, sexual orientation or disability.[28] The number of offences has fluctuated during the 1990s with a low number of such crimes, 69 occurring in 1990 and the high number, 143, occurring in 1996. In

2000, there were 134 hate crimes committed in Connecticut. The highest number of incidents were anti-black bias motivated.[29]

The *1998 Report* stated that, "If democracy is to persist and flourish, there must be a sense of the common good, a sense of collective ties beyond individual self-interest."[30] The benchmark of commonweal sought to examine the extent of community volunteerism and philanthropy within the state. The *1996 Report* cited that there were over 34,000 people volunteering their time in Connecticut agencies.[31] In 1995, the combined assets of over 1,000 Foundations in Connecticut represented $3.4 billion and foundations in Connecticut granted $206 million.[32]

Over the last two decades, its seems that discussions, not only in America, but on a global basis about civics and democratic participation, have become more widespread in both academic and political arenas. Most of these discussions are serious, sincere attempts to better understand the critical role individuals must play in a democratic society and how our involvement in the political institutions within that society can be enhanced and be opened to even greater participation. In the world of the classical Athenians, citizenship as active involvement in community life for the common good was the norm. It was a privileged status and carried with it much responsibility. These individuals perceived citizenship as self-fulfillment and their reward for participation was virtue. Much later in America, our nation's founders looked to the concept of active citizenship and public participation to support their arguments for the new Constitution of a new nation. This involvement would help to secure the distribution and separation of public power and provide a balance in government to check the emergence of tyranny. The individual freedoms outlined in the Constitution would be guaranteed through the processes of democratic participation. For Thomas Jefferson in particular, the notion of effective public participation could only be realized through the important process of education.

As this book has pointed out earlier, those who first settled in Connecticut were not very democratic as we might think of that term today. To the typical Puritan living in Connecticut, government and church co-existed to enhance and provide order for the community. Rule by the many was not considered the process by which order could be harmoniously achieved. Those few who governed civic affairs were those who held stature, wealth and religious standing within the community. But even at this early time, some of the practices of democratic government which today are still readily recognized, such as, voting, local control and a respect for written law were clearly evident. The political history of Connecticut from these early times to the present has been one of ever-expanding opportunity for individual participation in public life and ever-evolving government involvement in state and local public affairs.

Is Connecticut's state of democracy any better or any worse than any other state in America? The observations and information provided in this book have not attempted to measure Connecticut against other states. What they do reveal is that Connecticut is a state that is interested in measuring its own efforts in democracy; in identifying areas for enhancing and improving government and in providing the opportunities for its citizens to more fully participate in democratic life. This interest in itself is something that seems most fitting for the Constitution State and is something for all of its citizens to be proud of.

APPENDIX

Selected On-Line Sources of Interest

Connecticut History

University of Connecticut Library
http://www.lib.uconn.edu/cho

Connecticut Historical Society
http://www.chs.org/

Connecticut Maps
http://www.ct.gov/ecd

Teaching Resources
http://www.yale.edu/ynhti

Connecticut Municipal Government

Towns and Cities in Connecticut
http://www.state.ct.us/town.html

Connecticut Conference of Municipalities
http://www.ccm-ct.org/

Town Profiles
http://www.hickoryhill.com/

Connecticut Municipal Public Access Initiative
http://www.munic.state.ct.us/

Connecticut Courts and Criminal Matters

Connecticut Judicial Branch
http://www.jud.state.ct.us/ystday/history.html

The National Center for State Courts
http://www.ncsc.din.us/division/research/csp

Connecticut Chief State's Attorney
http://www.csao.state.ct.us/

The Connecticut Legislature

Connecticut's State Legislature, The General Assembly
http://www.cga.state.ct.us/

Connecticut Republican House Members
http://www.housegop.state.us/

Connecticut Republican Senate Members
http://www.senatereps.state.ct.us/

Connecticut Democratic House Members
http://www.cga.state.ct.us/hdo/

Connecticut Democratic Senate Members
http://www.senatedems.state.ct.us

Connecticut Legislature's Office of Fiscal Analysis
http://www.cga.state.ct.us/ofa/

Connecticut General Statutes
http://www.cslib.org/llru.htm

Elections and Campaigns

Campaign Finance
http://www.campaignfinancesite.org/

The Women's Campaign School at Yale University
http://www.wcsyale.org/

Election Statistics
http://www.sov-sots.state.ct.us/

The Alliance for Better Campaigns
http://www.bettercampaigns.org/

Government Offices and Departments

Connecticut State Register and Manual
http://www.sots.state.ct.us/RegisterManual/regman.htm

Most Connecticut state offices
http://www.state.ct.us/

Attorney General
http://www.cslib.org/attygenl/press

Governor's Office
http://www.state.ct.us/governor

Governor's Budget
http://www.opm.state.ct.us/publicat.htm

Secretary of the State
http://www.sots.state.ct.us/

Treasurer
http://www.state.ct.us.ott/

Comptroller
http://www.osc.state.ct.us/

Connecticut Department of Revenue Services
http://www.drs.state.ct.us/

Connecticut Department of Labor
http://www.ctdol.state.ct.us/

Connecticut Office of Policy and Management
http://www.opm.state.ct.us/

Connecticut Department of Public Safety
http://www.state.ct.us/dps

Connecticut Department of Public Health
http://www.state.ct.us/dph

Connecticut Department of Environmental Protection
http://www.dep.state.ct.us/

Connecticut Department of Education
http://www.state.ct.us/sde

Connecticut Political Parties

Republican Party
http://www.ctgop.org/

Democratic Party
http://www.dems.info/index.php

Green Party
http://www.ctgreens.org/

Libertarian Party
http://www.lpct.org/

Natural Law Party
http://www.natural-law.org/

Non-Governmental Public Interest Organizations

League of Women Voters of Connecticut
http://www.lwvct.org/

Connecticut Business and Industry Association
http://www.cbia.org/

Connecticut Education Association
http://www.cea.org/

Common Cause Connecticut
http://www.commoncause.org/states.connecticut

Connecticut Public Interest Research Group
http://www.connpirg.org/

Connecticut Coalition for Clean Air
http://www.sootysix.org

Study Circles Resource Center
http://www.studycircles.org

State Taxpayer Groups
http://www.ntu.org/

Sources of News and Current Events

The Hartford Courant
http://www.ctnow.com/

The New Haven Register
http://www.zwire.com/

The Journal Inquirer
http://www.zwire.com/site/news.fm?brd=985

The Connecticut Public Affairs Network
http://www.connecticutnetwork.orgw/

Endnotes

Chapter One

1. James Daugherty and Philip E. Curtis, *An Outline of Government in Connecticut*, 3rd Edition (The Connecticut General Assembly, The House Committee on Publications, 1949), 46-48.

2. Duane Lockard, *New England State Politics*, (Princeton: Princeton University Press, 1959), 5-6.

3. See Harold D. Lasswell, *Politics: Who Gets What, When, How,* New York: (The World Publishing Company, 1963).

4. Paul Donnelly, "Don't Rob Connecticut of a Congressman," *The Hartford Courant*, 3 January, 2001, p. A11, and Dan Haar, "State's Delegation to Shrink," *The Hartford Courant*, 29 December 2000, p. A15.

5. Daniel Duffy, *Congressional and State Legislative Redistricting*, Office of Legislative Research Report, Connecticut General Assembly, OLR Report 2000-R-0989, 20 October, 2000.

6. See Lisa Chedekel, "GOP Wants More Time to Redraw Lines," *The Hartford Courant*, 4 December , 2001, p. B2 and Christopher Keating, "House: Simmons, Johnson Win Key Congressional Races," *The Hartford Courant*, 6 November 2002, p. A1.

7. Charles Stannard, "Redrawn Districts Swap Some Voters," *The Hartford Courant*, (Shoreline-Greater New Haven Edition) 3 December, 2001, p. B3.

8. Kimberly W. Moy, "New Map May Alter Political Futures," *The Hartford Courant*, (New Britain-Southington Edition) 3 December, 2001, p. B3.

9. Ibid., B3.

10. Robert S. Kravchuk, "The 'New Connecticut': Lowell Weicker and the Process of Administrative Reform." *Public Administration Review*, July/August vol. 53, no. 4, (1993): 330-31.

11. Steven P. Lanza, "The Ups and Downs of the Connecticut Income Tax," *The Connecticut Economy*, vol. 9, no. 2, Spring (2001): 13 and Will McEachern, "Connecticut's Progressive Income Tax," *The Connecticut Economy*, vol. 6, no. 2, Spring (1998): 18-19.

12. John G. Rowland, *Governor Economic Report of the Governor of Connecticut, FY 2000-2001*, (February 2000), 113.

13. Connecticut Office of Policy and Management, *Municipal Fiscal Indicators*, 1995-1999, (October, 2000), A-6.

14. Connecticut Conference of Municipalities, *State Aid to Connecticut Cities and Towns: A CCM Analysis*, (January 2001), 7-8.

15. "Your Child's New Best Friend in Health Care," *Husky Healthcare for Uninsured Kids and Youth*, <http;// www. Huskyhealth.com/about.html> (12 July 2002).

16. Connecticut Department of Administrative Services, *Digest of Administrative Reports to the Governor*, vol. LIV, Hartford, CT : 1999, 131.

17. John G. Rowland, Governor, *Economic Report of the Governor, Connecticut, FY 2000-2001* (February 2000), 153.

18. Andrew Julien, "State Files Suit Against Four HMOs," *The Hartford Courant*, 8 September 2000, p. A8.

19. *The Hartford Courant*, "Agenda 2001," 31 December, 2000, p. C1.

20. Mark Miringoff, William Hoynes, Sandra Opdyke and Marque-Luisa Miringoff, "The Social State of Connecticut: 2001," (Tarrytown, New York: *Fordham Institute for Innovation in Social Policy, 2002*), 40.

21. C.E. Bower, F. A. Amadeo and L.M. Meuller. *One Hundred Fifty-First Connecticut Registration Report. For the Year Ended December 31, 1998.* (Hartford, CT: Connecticut Department of Public Health 2002), iii.

22. Michael K. Gallis and Associates, Connecticut Strategic Economic Framework: Defining the Issues, Relationships and Resources Necessary to Compete in a Global Economy. http://www.ctregionalinstitute.org cited in Vicki Gervickas, "Keep Connecticut Competitive in the Global Economy," *Construction*, vol. 39, no. 4, Winter (2000): 22.

23. Dennis R. Heffley and Steven P. Lanza, "Driving More?. . .Enjoying it Less?" *The Connecticut Economy*, vol. 7, no. 4, Fall (1999): 4.

24. Moira Lyons, "Transportation: The Time to Start is Now, *The Connecticut Economy*, vol. 9, no. 2, Spring (2001): 20.

25. Connecticut Department of Administrative Services, *The Digest of Administrative Reports to the Governor*, vol. LIV, 2000-01: 318.

26. Connecticut Secretary of the State, *Connecticut State Register and Manual 2001*, 248.

27. Connecticut Department of Administrative Services. *The Digest of Administrative Reports to the Governor*, vol. LII, (1998), 121.

28. *Digest of Administrative Reports*, (1999), 121.

29. "Connecticut Policy and Economic Foundation," *Connecticut Public Schools Guide*, (1999), 12.

30. Connecticut Department of Education, *Profiles of Our Schools: The Condition of Education in Connecticut, 1999-2000*, Theodore S. Sergi, Commission of Education, (2001), 3.

31. "Connecticut Policy and Economic Foundation." *Connecticut Public Schools Guide*, 7-10.

32. "Connecticut Department of Education," *Profiles of Our Schools*, 5.

33. Rick Green, "National Report Gives State's Schools B's for All But Equity," *The Hartford Courant*, 11 January 2001, p. A4.

34. Arthur W. Wright, "On This Roll of the Dice, Southeastern Connecticut (and the Rest of Us) Got Lucky," *The Connecticut Economy*, vol. 9, no. 1, Winter (2001): 12.

35. Ibid., 12-13.

36. *Economic Report of the Governor FY 2000-2001*, 128.

37. Lynn Bixby, "Thefts Feed A Casino Habit," *The Hartford Courant*, 22 August, 2000, p. A1.

38. Rick Green, "Gambling's Deepest Debts," *The Hartford Courant*, 11 March 2002, p. B1.

39. Miringoff, *The Social State of Connecticut*, 20-22.

40. Ibid., 40.

41. Connecticut Department of Public Safety, Division of State Police, Crimes Analysis Unit, *Crime in Connecticut 2000*, Annual Report of the Uniform Crime Reporting Program, (2000), 5.

42. Jon Lender and Mark Pazniokas , "3 Plead Guilty in Corruption Case," *The Hartford Courant*, 24 September 1999, p. A1.

43. Mike McIntire and Jon Lender, "Silvester Staffers Landed State Jobs," *The Hartford Courant*, 14 November, 1999, p. A13.

44. Edmond H. Mahony, "More Details on Giordano," *The Hartford Courant*, 19 September 2002, p. B1.

45. Mark Pazniokas and Janice D'arcy, "Wine, Gems and Cash," *The Hartford Courant*, 1 November 2001, p. A1.

46. Christopher Keating, "Senate Votes to Disband Sheriffs," *The Hartford Courant*, 13 April 2000, p. A3.

47. Between Boston and New York. *The Connecticut Experience Series* produced by *Connecticut Public Television* and the Connecticut Humanities Council, 1990, videocassette.

48. Elazar, Daniel. *American Federalism: A View From the States, 2ⁿᵈ Edition.* (New York: Thomas Y. Crowell Company, 1972), 89.

49. Michael J. Sandel, *Democracy's Discontent* (Cambridge: The Belknap Press of Harvard University Press. 1996), 4-5.

50. James·A. Marone, *The Democratic Wish* (New York: Basic Books, 1990), 17.

51. Daniel Elazar, 100-101.

52. Robert S. Erikson, John P. McIver, and Gerald C. Wright Jr. "State Political Culture and Public Opinion," *American Political Science Review*, 81 (1987): 797-99.

53. David C. Moon, John C. Pierce, and Nicholas Lovrich, "Political Culture in the Urban West: Is it Really Different?" *State and Local Government Review,* vol. 33, no. 3, Fall (2001): 198.

54. Clyde D. McKee, Jr., "Connecticut: A Political System in Transition," in *New England Political Parties*, ed. Josephine F. Milburn and William Doyle (Cambridge, MA: Schenkman Publishing Company, Inc., 1983), 65.

55. Jason Jakubowski, Correspondence to author. 22 June 2002.

Chapter 2

1. Hammond J. Trumbull, *Historical Notes on the Constitutions of Connecticut, 1639-1818,* (Hartford: The Case, Lockwood and Brainard Company, 1901), 8.

2. Christopher Collier, " The Connecticut Declaration of Rights Before the Constitution of 1818: A Victim of Revolutionary Redefinition," *Connecticut Law Review,* vol. 15, no. 1, Fall, (1982): 90.

3. Henry S. Cohn, *Connecticut Constitutional History 1636-1776,* Commissioned by the Museum of Connecticut History, 1988. <http://www.cslib.org/cts4c.htm>, (30 September 2002).

4. Wesley W. Horton, *The Connecticut State Constitution,* (Westport: Greenwood Press, 1993), 2.

5. See Deryck Collingwood, *Thomas Hooker 1586-1647, Father of American Democracy*, (Interlaken, New York: Heart of the Lakes Publishing, 1995.)

6. Albert E. Van Dusen, *Puritans Against the Wilderness: Connecticut History to 1763*, The Center for Connecticut Studies, Eastern Connecticut State College, vol. 1, (Chester, CT: The Pequot Press, 1975), 47.

7. Charles Henry Douglas. *The Government of the People of Connecticut,* (Philadelphia: Eldredge and Brother, 1896), 12.

8. William M. Maltbie, "The First Constitution of Connecticut," in Connecticut Secretary of the State. *Connecticut State Register and Manual*, 2001, 56.

9. Richard L. Bushman, *From Puritan to Yankee,* (Cambridge: Harvard University Press, 1967), 5.

10. Albert E. Van Dusen, *Connecticut*, (New York: Random House, 1961), 41.

11. Connecticut Secretary of the State, *Connecticut Register and Manual*, 2001, (Hartford, CT), 56-60.

12. Albert E. Van Dusen, *Puritans Against the Wilderness*, 36.

13. Simeon E. Baldwin, *History of Connecticut,* Edited by Morris Galpin Osborn, (New York: The States History Company, 1925), 9.

14. *Connecticut Register and Manual,* 2001, 56.

15. Norman LeVaun Stamps, *Political Parties in Connecticut 1789-1819*. (Ph.D. Dissertation, Yale University, Political Science, Yale University: New Haven, CT, 1968), 31.

16. Charles M. Andrews, *The Beginnings of Connecticut 1632-1662,* Tercentenary Commission of the State of Connecticut, (Yale University Press, 1934), 47.

17. Albert E. Van Dusen, *Puritans Against the Wilderness*, 37.

18. Collier, "The Connecticut Declaration of Rights Before the Constitution of 1818: A Victim of Revolutionary Redefinition," *Connecticut Law Review,* vol. 15, no. 1, Fall, (1992): 90 and Collier, Christopher." The Fundamental Orders of Connecticut and the American Constitution,." *Connecticut Law Review,* vol. 21, no. 4, Summer, (1989): 866.

19. Collier, Christopher." The Fundamental Orders of Connecticut and the American Constitution." *Connecticut Law Review,* vol. 21, no. 4, Summer, 1989: p. 868-869.

20. Albert E. Van Dusen, *Connecticut*, 42.

21. Andrews, *The Beginnings of Connecticut*, 47.

22. Bushman, *From Puritan to Yankee*, 9.

23. Margaret Richards, *350 Years of Connecticut Government: A Search for the Common Good, Teachers Handbook,* ed. Denise Wright Merrill, William Marcy, *Journal Activities,* Connecticut Consortium for Law and Citizenship Education, Inc., (1988), 47.

24. Albert E. Van Dusen, *Puritans Against the Wilderness,* 52-55.

25. Horton, *Connecticut Constitution,* 4.

26. Albert E. Van Dusen, *Puritans Against the Wilderness,* 69-71.

27. Horton, *Connecticut Constitution,* 4.

28. Margaret Richards, *350 Years,* 113.

29. Janice Law Trecker, *Preachers, Rebels and Traders, Connecticut 1818-1865,* vol. 3, Series in Connecticut History, (Chester: The Pequot Press, 1975), 47.

30. A.J. Beitzinger, *A History of American Political Thought,* (New York: Dodd, Mead and Company, 1972), 308.

31. Connecticut Secretary of the State, *Connecticut State Register and Manual,* 1952, State, Hartford, CT, 39.

32. Horton, 6.

33. Alan W. Brownsword, "The Constitution of 1818 and Political Afterthoughts, 1800-1840," *Connecticut Historical Society Bulletin,* vol. 30, no. 1. January (1965): 3.

34. Horton, 7.

35. Trumbull, 35-40.

36. Brownsword, 2.

37. Charles S. Grant, *Democracy in the Connecticut Frontier Town of Kent,* (New York: W.W. Norton & Company, Inc. 1972), 117.

38. Connecticut Secretary of the State, *Connecticut State Register and Manual 2002,* (Hartford, CT) 87-90.

39. Margaret Richards, 113.

40. Horton, 10-11.

41. Brownsword, 3.

42. Connecticut Secretary of the State, *Connecticut Register and Manual 1881,* (Hartford, CT: Brown and Gross, 1881), 209-225.

43. Brownsword, 7.

44. Connecticut Secretary of the State, *Connecticut Register and Manual 1952,* (Hartford, CT), 52-64.

45. Margaret Richards, 116.

46. Jane E. Zarem, ed. and compiler, *The Connecticut Citizen's Handbook, A Guide to State Government*, Third edition, League of Women Voters of Connecticut Education Fund. (Chester, CT, The Globe Pequot Press, 1987), 18.

47. Baker v. Carr 369 U.S. 186, (1962).

48. Gray v. Sanders. 372 U.S. 368, 381, (1963).

49. Westberry v. Sanders. 376 U.S. 1, (1964).

50. Reynolds v. Simms 377 U.S. 533, (1964).

51. Butterworth v. Dempsey, 237 F. Supp. 302 (D. Conn.); 378 U.S. 564, (1964).

52. John Dempsey, Governor. Address to the Convention, *Journal of the Constitutional Convention of Connecticut, 1965*. (Hartford: State of Connecticut, 1965), 7-8.

53. David Ogle. "The Modernization of the General Assembly" in *Perspectives of a State Legislature*. ed. Clyde D. McKee, Jr. (Hartford: Aetna Life and Casualty, 1978), 21.

54. Connecticut Advisory Commission on Intergovernmental Relations, *Home Rule in Connecticut: Its History, Status and Recommendations for Change*, (Hartford, CT, January 1987), 10-12.

55. Horton v. Meskill, 172 Conn. 615, (1977).

56. Thomas B. Mooney, *Practical Guide to Connecticut School Law*, Second Edition, (Wethersfield, CT: Connecticut Association of Boards of Education, Inc., 2000), 6.

57. Lawrence F. Cafero Jr., "Scrap the School Spending Formula and Start Over," *The Hartford Courant*, 23 February 2001, p. A19.

58. Sheff v. O'Neil, 238 Conn. 1, (1996) and Sheff v. O'Neil, 45 Conn. Sup. 630 (Superior Court, 3 March 1999).

59. Mooney, 6-8.

60. Ibid, 16.

61. Ibid, 21.

Chapter 3

1. Noah Webster, "A Brief History of Political Parties in the United States," Chapter XIX in *A Collection of Papers on Political, Literary, and Moral Subjects*, (New York: Webster and Clark. 1843), 334-335.

2. Sarah McCally Morehouse, *State Politics, Parties and Policy,* (New York: Holt, Rinehart and Winston, 1981), v.

3. Gary L. Rose, *Connecticut Politics at the Crossroads,* (Lanham: University Press of America, Inc., 1992), 30.

4. Norman L. Stamps, *Political Parties in Connecticut, 1789-1819,* (Ph.D. Dissertation, Yale University, New Haven: Yale University. 1950), 1.

5. Duane Lockard, *New England State Politics,* (Princeton: Princeton University Press. 1959), 229.

6. Ibid., 229.

7. Joseph I. Lieberman, *The Power Broker: A Biography of John M. Bailey, Modern Political Boss,* (Houghton Mifflin: Boston. 1966), 21.

8. Duane Lockard, 230.

9. Joseph I. Lieberman, *The Power Broker,* 22.

10. Secretary of the State of Connecticut, *Connecticut State Register and Manual 2001,* 82-83.

11. Duane Lockard, 245

12. Herbert F. Janick Jr., *A Diverse People: Connecticut 1914 to the Present,* Volume 5 in Series of Connecticut History, (Chester, CT: The Pequot Press. 1975), 26.

13. Joseph I. Lieberman, *The Power Broker,* 28-30.

14. Duane Lockard, 251.

15. Kevin F. Rennie, "Connecticut Swayed a Convention 60 Years Ago," *The Hartford Courant,* 28 July 2000, p. A19.

16. Joseph I. Lieberman, *The Power Broker,* 25.

17. Duane Lockard, 239-241.

18. Ibid., 250.

19. Joseph I. Lieberman, *The Power Broker,* p. 3.

20. Grant Reeher, *Narratives of Justice,* (Ann Arbor: University of Michigan Press. 1996), 219.

21. Michele Jacklin, "Democrats Cleaned GOP Clocks Statewide," *The Hartford Courant,* 15 November 2000, p. A15.

22. Robert Jackson, "Hartford Democrats—Party of the People," *The Hartford Courant,* 27 October 1999, p. A17.

23. Austin Ranney, "Parties in State Politics," in *Politics in the American States,* eds. Herbert Jacob and Kenneth N. Vines, (Boston: Little, Brown and Company, 1971), p. 87.

24. John F. Bibby, Cornelius Cotter, James L. Gibson and Robert Huckshorn. "Parties in State Politics" in *Politics in the American States*, 5th Edition, ed. Virginia Grey, Herbert Jacob and Robert B. Albritton (Glenview, Illinois: Scott, Foresman/Little, Brown Higher Education, 1990), 92.

25. Bibby, John F. and Holbrook, Thomas M. "Parties and Elections" in *Politics in the American State: A Comparative Analysis*, 7th edition , ed. Virginia Gray, Russell Hanson, and Herbert L. Jacob, (Washington, D.C.: CQ Press 1999), 93-96.

26. Clyde D. McKee, Jr. and Paul Peterson, "Connecticut: Party Politics as a Steady Habit," in *Parties and Politics in the New England States*, (Northeastern Political Science Association, Polity, Inc., 1997), 120-121.

27. Gary L. Rose, 5.

28. Ibid., 13.

29. Ibid., 72.

30. Ibid., 14-15.

31. Ibid., 95-96.

32. McKee and Peterson, 132.

33. Mary M. Janicki, "Background on Differences in Connecticut Primary Laws," Office of Legislative Research, Connecticut General Assembly, *OLR Research Report 2002-R-0142* (4 February 2002).

34. See Associated Press, "Plaintiffs Still Hopeful State Primary Law will be Thrown Out." *The Hartford Courant*, <http://ctnow.com/news/local/statewire/hc-26020800.PSA.M0916.bc—ct—primaug> (26 August 2002) and Elizabeth Daniel, "Statement on Decision in Campbell vs. Bysiewicz." Brennan Center for Justice at New York University School of Law, Press Center.<http://www.brennancenter.org/presscenter/pressrelease_2002_0805.html > (20 September 2002).

35. Tashjean v. Connecticut 479 U.S. 20, 1986.

36. Chris Depino, Class Lecture, University of Connecticut, 10/25/99.

37. Gary L. Rose, 74.

38. Joseph I. Lieberman, with Michael D'Orso, *In Praise of Public Life,* (New York: Simon & Schuster, 2000), 28.

39. Ibid., 43-44.

40. Jason Jakubowski, Class Lecture, University of Connecticut, 2001.

41. Grace E. Merritt, "Public Office Losing Luster," *The Hartford Courant*, 4 September 2001, p. B1.

42. McKee and Peterson, 132-133.

43. Secretary of the State of Connecticut, *Connecticut State Register and Manual 2000*, "Vote for State Senators, November 3, 1998, Senatorial Districts" and "Vote for State Representatives, November 3, 1998, Assembly Districts," 738-769.

44. Tom Swan, "What a Bargain!" *The Hartford Courant*, 4 March 2001, p. C1.

45. Edward D. Feigenbaum, J.D. and James A. Palmer, J.D., Federal Election Commission, "Campaign Finance Law 98: A Summary of State Campaign Finance Laws with Quick Reference Charts," <http://www.fec.gov/pages/cflaw98.html > (30 September 2002).

46. Common Cause Connecticut, "The Problem with Connecticut Elections," <http://www.commoncause.org/states/connecticut/election_problems2.html> (1997), (11 July 2000).

47. DeLuca, Louis C., "Why New Campaign Finance Laws? The System Already Works," *The Hartford Courant*, 22 October 1999, p. D15.

48. David Lightman, "Battle Over Soft Money is On," *The Hartford Courant*, 12 February 2002, p. A4.

49. Common Cause, "State Money & State Elections." <http://www.commoncause.org/states/softmoney_state.html> (1998), (23 August 2000).

50. "10 Questions for Jesse Ventura," *Time*, 29 April 2002, 8.

51. Paul S. Herrnson, and Ron Faucheux, "Outside Looking In: Views of Third Party and Independent Candidate," *Campaigns and Elections,* August, 1999, <http://www. Bsos.umd.edu/gvpt/herrnson/artart3html (30 September 2002).

52. Donald G. Ferree, "The Reform Party Prophet?" *The Public Perspective*, August/September, (1999): 5.

53. Connecticut Secretary of the State, "Registration and Party Enrollment Statistics as of October 24, 2000," <http://www.sots.state.ct.us.ElectionDivision Lists/enroll-minor.pdf> (30 September 2002).

54. Donald G. Ferree, 5-7.

Chapter 4

1. Joseph I. Lieberman, "Guidelines for Initiating Legislation and Understanding its Scope," in *Perspectives of a State Legislature*, ed. Clyde D. McKee Jr., (Hartford: Aetna Life and Casualty, 1978), 58-59.

2. Howard Klebanoff, "Legislative Oversight: The Neglected Legislative Function," in *Perspectives on a State Legislature*, ed. Clyde D. McKee, Jr. (Hartford: Aetna Life and Casualty, 1978), 97.

3. Connecticut Secretary of the State, *Connecticut Register and Manual 2001*, "The First Constitution of Connecticut," 56-60.

4. Clyde D. McKee, Jr., "Constitutional Principles and the Quest for Power," in *Perspectives on a State Legislature*, ed. Clyde D. McKee, Jr. (Hartford: Aetna Life and Casualty, 1978), 5.

5. Wesley W. Horton, *The Connecticut State Constitution,* (Westport: Greenwood Press, 1993), 14-15.

6. David Ogle, "The Modernization of the General Assembly," in *Perspectives of a State Legislature*, ed. Clyde D. McKee, Jr. (Hartford: Aetna Life and Casualty, 1978), 20.

7. Connecticut Secretary of the State, *Connecticut Register and Manual 1952*, 52.

8. Wesley W. Horton, 16-17.

9. David Broder, "State Legislatures Have Made Great Strides This Century," *The Hartford Courant*, 30 August 1999, p. A9.

10. David Ogle, 20-21.

11. Connecticut Office of Legislative Management, *Connecticut Legislative Guide*, 2000 Session, 174-175.

12. Grant Reeher, *Narratives of Justice,* (Ann Arbor: University of Michigan Press, 1996), 213.

13. Ibid., 207-226.

14. David Ogle, 23.

15. Jane E. Zarem, *The Connecticut Citizen's Handbook*, Third Edition, League of Women Voters Education Fund, (Chester: The Globe Pequot Press, 1987), 34.

16. Grant Reeher, 226-234.

17. Connecticut Office of Legislative Management, *Connecticut Legislative Guide 2000*, 177-180 and League of Women Voters of Connecticut, *How a Bill Becomes a Law in Connecticut* (undated).

18. Kathleen M. Rubenbauer, State of Connecticut, Office of Policy and Management, Presentation at the 58th Annual School for Assessors and Boards of Assessment Appeals, 21 June 2002.

19. Grant Reeher, 268-269.

20. Ibid., 203.

21. Gary L. Rose, *Connecticut at the Crossroads*, (Lanham: University Press of America, 1992), 41-42.

22. Connecticut Permanent Commission on the Status of Women, *Women of the New Millennium*, 2000 Annual Report, 23.

23. Connecticut Office of Legislative Management, *Legislative Guide*, 2000 p. 164.

24. Ibid., 166.

25. Ibid., 168.

26. Ibid., 168-169.

27. Robert Satter, *A Path in the Law* (Guilford, CT: The Connecticut Law Book Company, 1996), 204.

28. Grant Reeher, 227.

29. Sarah McCally Morehouse, "Connecticut Political Parties Court the Interest Groups," in *Interest Group Politics in the Northeastern States*, ed. Ronald J. Hrebenar and Thomas S. Clive (University Park: The Pennsylvania State University Press, 1993), 32-33.

30. Wayne R. Swanson, *Lawmaking in Connecticut*, The General Assembly, (New London: CT, Wayne R. Swanson, 1978), 73-74.

31. Duane Lockard, *New England State Politics* (Princeton: Princeton University Press. 1959), 286-287.

32. Connecticut Office of the Secretary of the State Miles S. Rapoport, *Report on the State of Democracy in Connecticut*, Second Biennial Report, (1998), 33.

33. Sarah McCally Morehouse, 32-33.

34. Lisa Chedekel, "Rowland Confidant's Firm Tops Lobby List," *The Hartford Courant*, 19 February 2002, p. B7.

35. See for example Connecticut Ethics Commission, *Outside Communicators: Fundamental Terms Communicators Registered for Two-Year Period Ending 12/31/2000*, 17 May 1999.

36. Lisa Chedekel, "Rowland Confidant's Firm Tops Lobby List," p. B7.

37. Christopher Keating, " 'Filthy Five' Plants Prevail." *The Hartford Courant*, 27 April 2000, p. A18.

38. The specific legislation is referred to as House Bill 5209 which the governor signed on May 2, 2002. See the Connecticut Coalition for Clean Air, *Clean Up the Sooty Six*, <http://www.sootysix.org/index.html> (13 November 2002).

39. See the mission statement of the Connecticut Conference of Municipalities, *General Assembly Handbook for Municipal Officials*, 2002 Edition, located on the back cover.

40. Daley, David. "Home Court Advantage," *Northeast (The Hartford Courant)*, 21 April 2002, 2.

Chapter 5

1. Robert S. Kravchuk, "The 'New Connecticut:' Lowell Weicker and the Process of Administrative Reform," *Public Administration Review,* July/August vol. 53, no. 4, (1993): 333.

2. U.S. Bureau of the Census, "State Government Employment Data, Connecticut State Government," (March 2000) <http://blue.census.gov/govs/apes/00stct.txt> (5 October 2002).

3. Larry Williams, "Now for the Hard Part: Governing," *The Hartford Courant*, 5 January 1995, p. A9.

4. Norman L. Stamps, *Political Parties in Connecticut, 1789-1819,* (Ph.D. Dissertation, Yale University, New Haven: Yale University, 1950), 36.

5. Thad. L. Beyle, "New Governors in Hard Economic and Political Times," in *Governors and Hard Times*, ed. Thad L. Beyle, (Wash. D.C.: CG Press, 1992), 7.

6. Russell D. Murphy, "Connecticut: Lowell P. Weicker, Jr., A Maverick in the Land of Steady Habits," in *Governors and Hard Times,* ed. Thad L. Beyle, (Washington DC.: CG Press, 1992), 68.

7. Robert S. Kravchuk, 333.

8. Charles R. Adrian, *Governing Our Fifty States and Their Communities,* (New York: McGraw Hill Book Company, 1972), 39.

9. Carol W. Lewis, *Making Choices for Connecticut*, (Storrs, CT: Institute of Public Service, University of Connecticut, 1984), 8.

10. Susan Bysiewicz, *Ella,* (Old Saybrook: Peregrine Press, 1984), 81.

11. Jon E. Purmont, "20 Years Later, We Remember Ella Grasso," *The Hartford Courant*, 5 February 2001, p. A9.

12. Connecticut Conference of Municipalities. *Connecticut's Spending Cap: What are the Facts?* (25 January 2000), 1.

13. Shelly Geballe, "Connecticut's Spending Cap." *Connecticut Voices for Children*, 21 June 2000 in *CT Budget Choices*, produced by Melville Charitable Trust. <http://www.med.yale.edu/childstudy/CTvoices> (28 October 2002).

14. Jeff Benedict, *Without Reservation,* (New York: Perennial Harper Collins Publishers, 2001), 221.

15. Ibid., 221-225.

16. Ibid., 244-249.

17. Robert S. Kravchuk, 333.

18. Ibid., 335-336.

19. Ibid., 334.

20. Lisa Chedekel, "Rowland Calls Special Session," *The Hartford Courant*, 24 October 2002, p. B1.

21. Charles R. Adrian, 40.

22. Herbert F Janick. Jr., *A Diverse People, Connecticut 1914 to the Present,* (Chester: The Pequot Press, 1975), 80.

23. Susan Bysiewicz, 109-111.

24. Joseph I. Lieberman, *The Legacy,* (Hartford: Spoonwood Press, 1981), 192.

25. Charles R. Adrian, 40.

26. Joseph I. Lieberman, *The Power Broker,* (Boston: Houghton Mifflin Company, 1966), 173.

27. Roger M. Dove, "America is Bereft of Political Leaders with Vision," *The Hartford Courant*, 16 June 1992, p. B9

28. Jon E. Purmont, "20 Years Later, We Remember Ella Grasso," *The Hartford Courant*, 5 February 2001, p. A9.

29. Susan Bysiewicz, 73.

30. Michelle Jacklin, "New Governor Vows 'No More' Fountain of Endless Favors," *The Hartford Courant*, 5 January 1995, p. A1, A8.

31. Governor John G. Rowland, Inaugural Address, 4 January 1995, *The Hartford Courant, 5 January 1995, p. A15.*

32. Christopher Keating, "Rowland's Ratings Overcome Setbacks," *The Hartford Courant*, 22 December 1999, p. A1.

33. Lisa Chedekel, "The Governor, Intimately," *Northeast Magazine,* (The Magazine of *The Hartford Courant*), 24 September 2000, p. 6.

34. Mike McIntire and Jon Lender, "Silvester Staffers Landed State Jobs," *The Hartford Courant*, 14 November 1999, p. A13.

35. Lisa Chedekel, "Governor Backs Compromise Deficit Plan," *The Hartford Courant*, 16 November 2001, p. B1, B9.

36. Lisa Chedekel and Eric M. Weiss, "Compromise to Offset Deficit Passes," *The Hartford Courant*, 17 November 2001, p. B1.

37. Mike Swift and Tom Puleo, "Two Egos, One Mess," *The Hartford Courant*, 13 June 1999, p. A12.

38. Quinnipiac College Poll, "Patriot's Deal Sacks Rowland's Approval. Connecticut Voters Reject Deal Before Teams Pulls Out." Doug Schwartz, Poll Director, <http://www.quinnipiac.edu/polls/> (Release 4 May 1999).

39. Governor John G. Rowland, Letter to Secretary of the State Susan Bysiewicz, May 5, 2000.

40. *The Associated Press*, "Connecticut Senate Passes Campaign Finance Reform Bill," 13 April 2000, <http://www.freedomforum.org/news/2000/04/2000/04-13-05asp> (11 July 2000).

41. Governor John G. Rowland, Letter to Secretary of the State Susan Bysiewicz, 5 May 2000.

42. Lisa Chedekel, "Rowland: Orders National Guard To Nuclear Plants; State Police on High Alert," *The Hartford Courant*, 30 October 2001, p. A1.

43. "Mr. Rowland's Phone Calls," *The Hartford Courant*, 5 October 2001, p. A12.

44. The Associated Press, "Rowland Copes With Difficult Times," *The Hartford Courant*, 26 November 2001, p. B3.

45. Lisa Chedekel, "The Governor, Intimately," 11.

46. Ibid., 8.

47. Jon Lender, "In Snow, Thou Shalt Have No Other Gov Before Me," *The Hartford Courant*, 7 March 2001, p. D1.

48. Keith M. Phaneuf, "Rowland Maintains Healthy Lead in Poll," *Journal Inquirer*, 14 February 2002, p. 5.

49. Ibid., p. 5

50. Robert L. Lorch, *State and Local Politics*, Sixth Edition, (Upper Saddle River: Prentice Hall, 2001), 119-120.

51. See Connecticut Attorney General's Office Press Releases: "Blumenthal Releases Names of More Than 400 Child Support Delinquents," (12/1/97); "Attorney General's Statement on Bureau of Indian Affairs' Decision to Recognize an Eastern Pequot Tribe," (6/24/02); "Attorney General Hails $20 Million Fine Against R.J. Reynolds for Violating Terms of the 1998 National Tobacco Settlement," (6/6/02) <http://www.cslib.org/attygeneral press> (12 July 2002).

52. Secretary of the State of Connecticut, *Connecticut State Register and Manual 2001*, 93.

53. Ibid., 90.

54. Christopher B. Burnham, "The State Treasury Needs A Board of Trustees," *The Hartford Courant*, 14 September 1999, p. A13.

Chapter 6

1. *Connecticut Rules of Court, State and Federal*, "Code of Judicial Conduct," (West Group, 2000), 395.

2. Connecticut Judicial Branch, "Role of the Connecticut Courts," <http://www.jud.ct.us/ystday/role.html> (27 November 2001).

3. Connecticut Judicial Branch, *Connecticut Courts*, (1999), 8.

4. State of Connecticut Judicial Branch, "History of the Courts," <http://www.jud.state.ct.us/ystday/history.html>, (8 October 2002).

5. *Connecticut Courts*, 31-34.

6. Ibid., 34.

7. Ibid., 35.

8. State of Connecticut Judicial Branch, Connecticut Superior Court, Windham Judicial District, *Your Guide to Jury Duty*, April (1995), 6.

9. *Connecticut Courts*, 15.

10. The National Center for State Courts, "State Court Caseload Statistics, 2001," Table 15, "Felony Caseload in State Trial Courts of General Jurisdiction, 1991-2000," p. 190 and Table 16, "Tort Caseload in State Trial Courts of General Jurisdiction, 1991-2000," p. 194. <http://www.ncsconline.org/D_Research/csp/2001_Files/2001_sccs.html>, (8 October 2002).

11. Connecticut Department of Public Safety, Division of State Police, *Crime In Connecticut 2000*, Annual Report of the Uniform Crime Reporting Program, (2000), 5.

12. State of Connecticut, Division of Criminal Justice, "Prosecution in Connecticut: A Brief History,".<http://www.csao.state.us/whowereare.html>, (9 July 2002).

13. *Connecticut Courts*, 17.

14. Tom Condon, "Judging Scheinblum," *Northeast, (The Hartford Courant)*, 18 March 2001, p. 6.

15. Connecticut Judicial Branch, The Commission on Official Legal Publications, *Directory of the Connecticut Judicial Branch*, September, 1997, 101.

16. Jane E. Zarem, Editor and Compiler, *Connecticut Citizens Handbook League of Women Voters*, (Chester, CT : Globe Pequot Press, 1984), 62-63.

17. *Connecticut Courts*, 23.

18. See the Connecticut Constitution, Article Fifth, Section 2; Article XI of the Amendments; Article XX of the Amendments.

19. The National Center for State Courts, "State Court Caseload Statistics," for 2001, 1999-00, 1998, The Court Statistics Project, <http://www.ncsonline. org>, (October 8, 2002).

20. *Connecticut Rules of Court*, 395-401.

21. Leydon v. Greenwich 257 Conn. 318 (2001), see also Connecticut Conference of Municipalities, *Municipal Management Bulletin*, "Leydon v. Greenwich Exclusion of Non-Residents from Town Beach Held Unconstitutional; Ruling Applies to All Municipal Parks," 2 October 2001, No. 01-19.

22. State v. Troupe 237 Conn. 284 (1996) see also Jamie Mills, "Connecticut Supreme Court Limits Constancy of Accusation," Connecticut Sexual Assault Crisis Services, Inc, <http://www.connsacs.org/constanc.html> (6 January 2000).

23. Charles v. Charles 243 Conn. 255 (1997); see also Nicole Schiavi, "Supreme Court Rules Pequots Can Be Sued Individually in State Courts," *The News-Times*, 11 November 1997. <http://www.newstimes.com/archive97/ nov1197/rgd.html> (6 January 2000).

24. Town of Orange v. Modern Cigarette, Inc. 256 Conn. 557, (2001).

Chapter 7

1. Thomas Jefferson, Letter to Samuel Kercheval, 13 July 1816. Quoted in A.T. Mason, *Free Government in the Making*, 2nd Edition, (New York: Oxford University Press, 1956), 372. Quoted in the Advisory Commission on Intergovernmental Relations, *Citizen Participation in the American Federal System*. (Wash, D.C., 1980), 26.

2. Connecticut Office of Policy and Management, *Municipal Fiscal Indicators, 1995-1999*. October, 2000, A-7.

3. Worcester v. Worcester Consolidated Railway Company. (196 U.S. 539, 1905).

4. Willard v. Warden 8 Conn. 247, (1830).

5. Willimantic School Society v. First School Society in Windham, 14 Conn. 457, (1841).

6. State Ex. Rel. Bulkeley v. Williams, 86 Conn. 131, (1896).

7. City of Clinton v. Cedar Rapids and Missouri River Rail Road Company, 24 Iowa 455, (1868).

8. See John F. Dillon, Commentaries on the Law of Municipal Corporations, Fifth Edition, (Boston: Little, Brown. Section 237. 1911), quoted in Connecticut Advisory Commission on Intergovernmental Relations, *Home Rule in Connecticut*, Hartford, CT (January 1987), 3-4.

9. See Janice C. Griffith, "Connecticut's Home Rule: The Judicial Resolution of State and Local Conflicts," *University of Bridgeport Law Review*, 1983, used with permission and cited in Connecticut Advisory Commission on Intergovernmental Relations, *Home Rule in Connecticut: Its History, Status, and Recommendations for Change.* January 1987, 10-12.

10. Connecticut Advisory Commission on Intergovernmental Relations, *Home Rule in Connecticut*, (1987), 14-15.

11. Ibid., 17.

12. Shelton v. Commissioner of the Department of Environmental Protection 193 Conn. 506, 520-23.

13. Horton, Wesley W. *The Connecticut State Constitution,* (Westport: Greenwood Press, 1993), 153.

14. Hollister, Timothy S. "The Myth and Reality of Home Rule Powers in Connecticut," *Connecticut Bar Journal*, vol 59, (1985): 390.

15. Samual S. Cross, "Home Rule-Organic Law or Legislative Chimera?" *Connecticut Bar Journal*, vol. 58. (1984): 210.

16. Bryan A. Garner, Editor in Chief, *Black's Law Dictionary,* Abridged Seventh Edition. (Westgroup, St. Paul, Minnesota, 2000), s.v. "charter."

17. George Hill, *Connecticut Municipal Government,* (Storrs, CT: The Institute of Public Service, University of Connecticut, 1998), 3.

18. This table is based upon United States Bureau of the Census, 2000, "Geographic Comparison Table" Census 2000 Redistricting Data (Public Law 94-171) Summary File, Connecticut, Place and County Subdivision, http://factfinder.census.gov/bf/_lang=en_vt_name=DEC-2000_PL_U_GCTPL_geo_id=04000US09.htm (20 April 2002) and Frank B. Connolly, *Local Government in Connecticut*, 2nd Edition, Connecticut Conference of Municipalities, 2001, New Haven, Connecticut.

19. Frank B. Connolly, *Local Government in Connecticut*, 97.

20. Max R. White, "The Office of Selectman" in *Handbook for Connecticut Selectmen*, George E. Hill, (Storrs, CT: The Institute of Public Service, University of Connecticut, 1998), 2.

21. Richard L. Bushman, From Puritan to Yankee, (Cambridge: Harvard University Press, 1967), 36.

22. Max R. White, "The Office of Selectman," 2.

23. Connecticut Conference of Municipalities, *CCM Survey of Municipal Officials' Salaries Fiscal Year 1998-99*, 1999 Edition, New Haven, Connecticut, 1999, 25

24. Max R. White, "The Office of Selectman," 5.

25. George Hill, *Connecticut Municipal Government* (Storrs, CT: Institute of Public Service, Storrs: University of Connecticut, 1998), 4.

26. Board of Education of Naugatuck v. Town and Borough of Naugatuck, 70 Conn. App. 358, (2002)

27. George Hill, *Connecticut Municipal Government*, 8.

28. Frank Connolly, 28.

29. Citizens Research Education Network, *Inside City Hall: A Guide to the Hartford City Council*. David Desiderato, Executive Director CREN, Hartford, CT, May 1991, 2.

30. George Hill, *Connecticut Municipal Government*, 14-15.

31. Ibid., 15.

32. Tom Condon, "Ex-Mayor Says System Doesn't Work," T*he Hartford Courant*, 28 November 1999, B1.

33. George Hill, *Connecticut Municipal Government*, 16-17.

34. Robert Dahl, *Who Governs?* (New Haven: Yale University Press, 1961), 204.

35. Dannel P. Malloy, "Stamford's Example: A Formula for Success," *The Hartford Courant*, 21 March 1999, p. C1, C4.

36. Frank Connolly, *Local Government in Connecticut*, 97.

37. George Hill, *Connecticut Municipal Government*, 12.

38. Town of Simsbury, Connecticut, Simsbury Town Manager Study Committee, *Report to the Board of Selectmen*, April 1997, 17.

39. Gene Shipman, interview by Elissa Papirno, *The Hartford Courant*, 19 January 1992, C4.

40. George Hill, *Handbook for Connecticut Boards of Finance*, (Storrs, CT: Institute of Public Service: The University of Connecticut, 1992), 11.

41. Sandra Norman-Eady, Office of Legislative Research, Connecticut General Assembly, "Special Districts," *OLR Report 93-R-0739*, 20 October 1993.

42. Silas Andros, Compiler, *The Blue Laws*, (UConn Co-op: Bibliopola Press, University Press of New England, 1999), 91.

43. Jane E. Zarem, Compiler and Editor, *The Connecticut Citizen's Handbook*,

Third Edition, League of Women Voters Education Fund, (Chester: The Globe Pequot Press, 1987), 85-88.

44. Horton v. Meskill 172 Conn. 615 (1977).

45. Thomas B. Mooney, *A Practical Guide to Connecticut School Law*, Second Edition, (Connecticut Association of Boards of Education, Inc. Wethersfield, Connecticut, 2000), 73-74.

46. Connecticut Conference of Municipalities, *Increasing the State's Share of the Cost of Local Public Education: Connecticut's Challenge in Education Finance*, November, (1998), 2.

47. Connecticut Conference of Municipalities, *State Aid to Connecticut Cities and Towns, A CCM Analysis*. January, 2001, 9-10.

48. Thomas B. Mooney, *A Practical Guide. . .* 365.

49. Ibid., 77.

50. Ibid., 387.

51. Ibid., 24.

52. Connecticut Department of Education, *Profiles of Our Schools: The Condition of Education in Connecticut, 1999-2000*, Theodore S. Sergi, Commissioner of Education, 2001, 1.

53. John Rappa, *History of Connecticut's Boroughs*, Office of Legislative Research, Connecticut General Assembly, June 12, 1998, *OLR Report 98-R-0660.*

54. Connecticut Policy and Economic Council, Inc. "Municipalities Holding the Line on Spending and Tax Growth," *CPEC Review*, vol. 1, no. 3 April (1997), 6. http://www.cpec.org/review/9704review/9704review.html (19 July 2000).

55. Rosaline Levenson, *County Government in Connecticut, Its History and Demise,* (Storrs, CT: Institute of Public Service, University of Connecticut. 1981), 1.

56. Ibid., 34-40.

57. Ibid., 80-82.

58. Ibid., 91-94.

59. Ibid., 105.

60. Ibid., 118-120.

61. Connecticut Secretary of the State, *State Register and Manual 2001*, "Vote for Proposed Constitutional Amendment, 7 November 2000," 766-769.

62. Brian E. West and Don DeFronzo, Connecticut Advisory Commission on

Intergovernmental Relations, *Local Government Cooperative Ventures in Connecticut*, June (1996), 1.

63. Connecticut Advisory Commission on Intergovernmental Relations, *Local Government Cooperative Ventures in Connecticut*, 3.

64. Connecticut Advisory Commission on Intergovernmental Relations, *Local Government Cooperative Ventures in Connecticut*, 73.

65. Capital Region Council of Government, *Celebrating 30 Years of Regional Solutions to Regional Challenges, 1968-1998,* Annual Report. Fiscal Year 1998, 1.

66. Jefferson B. Davis, "The Need for Regional Thinking," *Connecticut Government*, Storrs, CT: Institute of Public Service, University of Connecticut, vol. 41, no. 1. Winter/Spring (1995), 2-4.

67. Leigh Standish, "Regionalism: An Unfair, Unworkable Model," *The Hartford Courant*, 5 February 2002, p. A9.

68. Judith Freedman, "Regionalism: A Local Decision," *Connecticut Government*, Storrs, CT: Institute of Public Service, University of Connecticut. vol. 41, no. 1, Winter/Spring (1995), 2.

Chapter 8

1. Leslie Brett, Executive Director, Permanent Commission on the Status of Women. Quoted in the Secretary of the State of Connecticut *Report on the State of Democracy in Connecticut 1998*, Second Biennial Report, (1998), 32.

2. The 1996 State of Democracy Advisory Board was composed of: Peter Bartucca, Leslie Brett, John Britain, Walter S. Brooks, Marc Caplan, Joel Cogen, Tom Corrigan, Joseph Courtney, Jefferson Davis, Rebecca Doty, Cathy Ehrhardt, Diane Evans, Juan Figueroa, Joseph Grabarz, Lynn Ide, Bernard Kavaler, Eugene Leach, Eric Lorenzini, T. Joseph Loy, Martha McCoy, James Miller, Merrilee Milstein, Richard Moorton, Jr., Antonia Moran, Nick Nyhart, Paul Petterson, Miles S. Rapport, Howard Reiter, Jean Rexford, Rosaido Rosario, Americo Santiago, Edward Sembor, Peggy Shanks and Ronald Taylor.

3. Connecticut Secretary of the State, *Report on the State of Democracy in Connecticut*, (Hartford, 1996), 3.

4. Edward C. Sembor, "On Knowledge and Interest," *Connecticut Government*, vol. 42, no. 1, Institute of Public Service, University of Connecticut, Winter /Spring (1997): 1.

5. Connecticut Secretary of the State, *Report on the State of Democracy in Connecticut*, Second Biennial Report, (Hartford, 1998), 20-21.

6. Quinnipiac College Poll, "Generation X-ers Show Lower Interest in Politics than Boomers and Mature Generations," Doug Schwartz, Poll Director, <http://www.quinnipiac.edu./polls/> (Release 26 October 1999).

7. Connecticut Secretary of the State, *Report on the State of Democracy in Connecticut*, (Hartford, 1996), 20.

8. *Report on the State of Democracy in Connecticut*, 1998, 26.

9. This data was compiled from Connecticut Secretary of the State, "Election Day Registration and Turnout," *State of Connecticut Register and Manual* for years 1990, 1992, 1994, 1996, 1998, 2000.

10. *Report on the State of Democracy in Connecticut*, 1996, 29.

11. Richard J. Porth, "Our Commonweal." Connecticut Government, vol. 42, no. 1, Institute of Public Service, University of Connecticut, Winter/ Spring (1997): 7.

12. Edward C. Sembor, "Building Community Citizenship Through Study Circles," *Public Management*, vol. 74, no. 6, June (1992): 15-17.

13. Leslie J. Brett, "On Social and Economic Equality and Opportunity." Connecticut Government, Institute of Public Service, University of Connecticut. vol. 42. no. 1, Winter/Spring (1997): 3.

14. *Report on the State of Democracy in Connecticut*, 1996, 37.

15. Mark Miringoff, William Hoynes, Sandra Opdycke and Marque-Luisa Miringoff, *The Social State of Connecticut*, 2001 (Tarrytown, New York: Fordham Institute for Innovation in Social Policy, 2001), 36.

16. Miringoff et. al., 39.

17. *Report on the State of Democracy in Connecticut*, 1998, 53.

18. Mike Swift, "Poverty's Web Widens," *The Hartford Courant*, 22 May 2002, A1.

19. *Report on the State of Democracy in Connecticut*, 1998, 53.

20. Miringoff et. al., 46.

21. Connecticut Conference of Municipalities, "Connecticut: A Tale of Two States," Connecticut Town and City, vol. 29, no. 3, (May-June 2001): 13.

22. Connecticut Conference of Municipalities, "Connecticut: A Tale of Two States," *Connecticut Town and City*, vol. 29, no. 6, November-December (2001): 10.

23. Connecticut Conference of Municipalities, "Connecticut: A Tale of Two

States," *Connecticut Town and City*, vol. 29, no. 5, September-October (2001): 14.

24. Mike Swift, "Poverty's Web Widens," *The Hartford Courant*, 22 May 2002, p. A12.

25. Connecticut Conference of Municipalities, *Connecticut Town and City*, Sept.-Oct. 2001, 14.

26. *Report on the State of Democracy in Connecticut*, 1998, 58-59.

27. Office of the Secretary of the State of Connecticut, *Gender and Racial Diversity on Connecticut State Appointive Bodies,* 1999, March (2000), ii-iii.

28. Connecticut Department of Public Safety, Division of State Police, Crimes Analysis Unit, Annual Report of the Uniform Crime Reporting Program, *Crime in Connecticut*, (2000), 325.

29. *Crime in Connecticut*, 325-26.

30. *Report on the State of Democracy in Connecticut*, 1998, 68.

31. Connecticut Secretary of the State, *Report on the State of Democracy in Connecticut*, 1996, 53.

32. Coordinating Council for Foundations, "Connecticut Giving Facts," 85 Gillett Street, Hartford, CT (1995).

BIBLIOGRAPHY

Adrian, Charles R. *Governing Our Fifty States and Their Communities,*. New York: McGraw Hill Book Company, 1972.

Andrews, Charles M. The Beginnings of Connecticut, 1632-1662, *Tercentenary Commission of the State of Connecticut*, Yale University Press, 1934.

Andrus, Silas. Compiler, *The Blue Laws*, University of Connecticut Co-op, The Bibliopola Press, University Press of New England, revised 1999.

Associated Press. "Plaintiffs Still Hopeful State Primary Law Will be Thrown Out," *The Hartford Courant*, <http://ctnow.com/news/local/statewire/hc-26020800.PSA.M0916.bc—ct—primaug26.story> (26 August 2002).

Associated Press. "Connecticut Senate Passes Campaign Finance Reform Bill," 13 April 2000, <http://www.freedomforum.org/news/2000/04/2000/04-13-05asp> (11 July 2000).

Associated Press. "Rowland Copes with Difficult Times," *The Hartford Courant*, 26 November 2001, p. B3.

Baldwin, Simeon E. History of Connecticut, Vol. I and II, ed. Morris Galpin Osborn, New York: The States History Company, 1925.

Beitzinger, A.J. *A History of American Political Thought*, New York: Dodd, Mead and Company, 1972.

Benedict, Jeff. *Without Reservation*, New York: Perennial Harper Collins Publishers, 2001.

Between Boston and New York. *The Connecticut Experience Series* produced by *Connecticut Public Televisio*n and the Connecticut Humanities Council, 1990, videocassette.

Beyle, Thad L. "New Governors in Hard Economic and Political Times."

In Beyle, Thad L. Editor, *Governors and Hard Times*, Washington D.C., CQ Press, 1992, 1-14.

Bibby, John F., Cornelius Cotter, James L. Gibson and Robert Huckshorn. "Parties in State Politics," in *Politics in the American States,* 5th Edition, ed. Virginia Grey, Herbert Jacob and Robert B. Albritton, Glenview, Illinois: Scott, Foresman/Little, Brown Higher Education, 1990, 85-122.

Bibby, John F. and Thomas M. Holbrook. "Parties and Elections," in *Politics in the American State: A Comparative Analsysis,* 7th edition, edited by Virginia Gray, Russell L. Hanson, Herbert Jacob, 93-96, CQ Press: Washington D.C., 1999, 66-112.

Bixby, Lynn. "Thefts Feed A Casino Habit." *The Hartford Courant*, 22 August 2000, p. A1.

Black's Law Dictionary. Abridged Seventh Edition, Bryan A. Garner, Editor in Chief, St. Paul, Minnesota: Westgroup, 2000.

Bollier, David. *Crusaders and Criminal, Victims and Visionaries*, Hartford, CT: Office of Attorney General Joseph I. Lieberman, 1986.

Bower, C.E., F.A. Amadeo, and L.M. Mueller. *One Hundred-Fifty First Registration Report for the Year Ended December 31, 1998*, Hartford, CT: Connecticut Department of Public Health.

Brett, Leslie J. "On Social and Economic Equality and Opportunity," *Connecticut Government*, Institute of Public Service, University of Connecticut, vol. 42, no. 1, Winter/Spring, (1997): 3-4.

Broder, David. "State Legislatures Have Made Great Strides This Century," *The Hartford Courant*, 30 August 1999, p. A9.

Brownsword, Alan. W. "The Constitution of 1818 and Political Afterthoughts 1800-1840," *Connecticut Historical Society Bulletin,*. vol. 30, no. 1, January (1965): 1-10.

Bushman, Richard L. *From Puritan to Yankee*, Cambridge: Harvard University Press, 1967.

Bysiewicz, Susan. *Ella*, Old Saybrook, CT: Peregrine Press, 1984.

Cafero, Lawrence F. Jr. "Scrap the Spending Formula and Start Over." *The Hartford Courant*, 23 February 2001, p. A19.

Capital Region Council of Government (CROG) Annual Report, 1998.

Chedekel, Lisa. "GOP Wants More Time to Redraw Lines," *The Hartford Courant*, 4 December 2001, p. B2.

Chedekel, Lisa. "Rowland Confidant's Firm Tops Lobby List." *The Hartford Courant*, 19 February 2002, p. B7.

Chedekel, Lisa. "The Governor, Intimately," *Northeast*, the magazine of *The Hartford Courant*, 24 September 2000, p. 5-13.

Chedekel, Lisa. "Rowland Calls Special Session," *The Hartford Courant*, 24 October 2001, p. B1.

Chedekel, Lisa. "Governor Backs Compromise Deficit Plan." *The Hartford Courant*, 16 November 2001, p. B1, B9.

Chedekel, Lisa and Eric M. Weiss. "Compromise to Offset Deficit Passes." *The Hartford Courant*, 17 November 2001, p. B1.

Chedekel, Lisa. "Rowland: Orders National Guard to Nuclear Plants; State Police on High Alert," *The Hartford Courant*, 30 October 2001, p. A1.

Citizens Research Education Network. *Inside City Hall, A Guide to the Hartford City Council*, May 1991.

Cohn, Henry S. "Connecticut Constitutional History 1636-1776," Commissioned by the Museum of Connecticut History, 1988. <http://www.cslib.org/cts4c.html> 30 September 2002.

Collier, Christopher. "The Connecticut Declaration of Rights Before the Constitution of 1818: A Victim of Revolutionary Redefinition," *Connecticut Law Review*, vol. 15, no.1, Fall, (1982): 87-98.

Collier, Christopher. "The Fundamental Orders of Connecticut and the American Constitution," *Connecticut Law Review*, vol. 21, no. 4. Summer (1989): 863-869.

Collingwood, Deryck. *Thomas Hooker 1586-1647, Father of American Democracy*, Heart of the Lakes Publishing: Interlaken, New York, 1995.

Common Cause Connecticut. "The Problem with Connecticut Elections." <http://www.commoncause.org/states/connecticut/election_problems2.html> (29 October 2002).

Common Cause. "Soft Money and State Elections." <http://www.commoncause.org/states/softmoney_state.html> (28 October 2002).

Connecticut Department of Administrative Services. *The Digest of Ad-*

ministrative Reports to the Governor 1999, John G. Rowland, Governor, Vol. LIII, Hartford, Connecticut, John McKay, Editor.

Connecticut Department of Administrative Services. *The Digest of Administrative Reports to the Governor 2000*, John G. Rowland, Governor, Vol. LIV, Hartford, Connecticut, John McKay and Cindy Duberek, Editors.

Connecticut Department of Administrative Services. *The Digest of Administrative Reports to the Governor 1998*, John G. Rowland, Governor, Vol. LII, Hartford, John McKay, Editor.

Connecticut Advisory Commission on Intergovernmental Relations. *Local Government Cooperative Ventures in Connecticut*, June 1996.

Connecticut Advisory Commission on Intergovernmental Relations. *Home Rule in Connecticut: Its History, Status and Recommendations for Change*. January 1987.

Connecticut Coalition for Clean Air. *Clean up the Sooty Six*, <http://www.sootysix.org/index.html> (13 November 2002).

Connecticut Conference of Municipalities. *State Aid to Connecticut Cities and Towns*, A CCM Analysis, January, 2001.

Connecticut Conference of Municipalities. *Municipal Salary Survey*, 1999.

Connecticut Conference of Municipalities. *Connecticut's Spending Cap: What are the Facts?* January 25, 2000.

Connecticut Conference of Municipalities. *Report: Connecticut's ECS Formula-Changes Since 1988*, September, 1997.

Connecticut Conference of Municipalities Handbook, 1997.

Connecticut Conference of Municipalities. *General Assembly Handbook for Municipal Officials,* 2002 Edition, New Haven, CT, 2002.

Connecticut Conference of Municipalities. "Connecticut: A Tale of Two States," *Connecticut Town and City,* vol. 29, no. 3, May-June (2001):13.

Connecticut Conference of Municipalities. "Connecticut: A Tal of Two States," *Connecticut Town and City,* vol. 29, no. 6, November-December 2001, 10.

Connecticut Conference of Municipalities. "Connecticut: A Tale of Two States." *Connecticut Town and City*, vol. 29, no. 5, September-October 2001, 14.

Connecticut Department of Education. *Profiles of Our Schools: The Condition of Education in Connecticut, 1999-2000*, Theodore S. Sergi, Commissioner, Hartford, CT, 2001.

Connecticut Ethics Commission. *Outside Communicators: Fundamental Terms: Communicators Registered for the Two Year Period Ending December 31, 2000.*

Connecticut General Assembly. Office of Legislative Management., *Connecticut Legislative Guide 2000.*

Connecticut Governor's Office. *Economic Report of the Governor FY 2000-2001.* John G. Rowland, Governor, February, 2000.

Connecticut Humanities Council. *Between Boston and New York*, the Connecticut Experience Series, produced with *Connecticut Public Television*, 1990, videocassette.

Connecticut Judicial Branch. *Connecticut's Courts*, 1999.

Connecticut Judicial Branch. Connecticut Superior Court, Windham Judicial District, *Your Guide to Jury Duty*, April, 1995.

Connecticut Policy and Economic Council. *Public Schools Guide*, 1999.

Connecticut Policy and Economic Council. "Municipalities Holding the Line on Spending and Tax Growth," *CPEC Review,* vol. 1, no. 3, April, (1997), 6, <http://www.cpec.org/review/9704review.html> (19 July 2000).

Connecticut Office of Policy and Management. Intergovernmental Policy Division, *Municipal Fiscal Indicators, Fiscal Years Ended 1995-1999*, October, 2000.

Connecticut Department of Public Health. *One Hundred Fifty-First Connecticut Registration Report, Births, Deaths, Marriages, Divorces 1998*, complied by C.E. Bower, F.A. Amadeo and L.M. Mueller, Hartford, CT, 2002.

Connecticut Department of Public Safety. Division of State Police, Crimes Analysis Unit, *Crime in Connecticut*, Annual Report of the Uniform Crime Reporting Program, 2000.

Connecticut Rules of Court, State and Federal. West Group, 2000.

Connecticut Secretary of the State, *Report on the State of Democracy in Connecticut*, 1996.

Connecticut Secretary of the State, Report on the State of Democracy in Connecticut, *Second Biennial Report*, 1998.

Connecticut Secretary of the State. "Vote for Proposed Constitutional Amendment, November 7, 2000," *Connecticut State Register and Manual*, 2001.

Connecticut Secretary of the State. *Gender and Racial Diversity on Connecticut State Appointive Bodies*, 1999.

Connecticut Secretary of the State. *Connecticut State Register and Manual,* 1881, Hartford, CT: Brown and Gross, 1881.

Connecticut Secretary of the State. *Connecticut State Register and Manual,* 1952, Hartford, CT, 1952.

Connecticut Secretary of the State. *Connecticut State Register and Manual,* 1998, Hartford, CT, 1998.

Connecticut Secretary of the State. *Connecticut State Register and Manual,* 2001, Hartford, CT, 2001.

Connecticut Secretary of the State. Connecticut State Register and Manual 2002. Hartford, CT, 2002.

Connecticut Secretary of the State. *Report on the State of Democracy in Connecticut,* Hartford, CT, 1996.

Connecticut Secretary of the State. *Report on the State of Democracy in Connecticut*, Second Biennial Report, Hartford, CT, 1998.

Connecticut Secretary of the State. *2000 Youth State of Democracy Report*, Hartford, CT, 2000.

Connecticut Secretary of the State. "Election Day Registration and Turnout," *Connecticut Register and Manual* for years: 1990, 1992, 1994, 1996, 1998, 2000.

Connecticut Secretary of the State. *Gender and Racial Diversity on Connecticut State Appointive Bodies,* 1999, March, 2000.

Connecticut Secretary of the State. "Vote for State Senators, November 3, 1998 Senatorial Districts" and "Vote for State Representatives, November 3, 1998 Assembly Districts," *State of Connecticut Register and Manual,* 2000, 738-769.

Connolly, Frank. *Local Government in Connecticut,* Second Edition, New Haven: Connecticut Conference of Municipalities, 2001.

Coordinating Council for Foundations. *Connecticut Giving Facts*, 1995.

Cross Samuel S. "Home Rule: Organic Law or Legislative Chimera?" *Connecticut Bar Journal,* vol. 58, (1984): 185-212.

Dahl, Robert A. *Who Governs?* New Haven: Yale University Press, 1961.

Daley, David. "Home Court Advantage," *Northeast, The Hartford Courant*, 21 April 2002, p. 2.

Daniel, Elizabeth. "Statement on Decision in Campbell v. Bysiewicz." Brennan Center for Justice at New York University School of Law, Press Center, <http://www.brennancenter.org/presscenter/pressrelease_2002_0805.html> (3 October 2002).

Daugherty, James and Philip E. Curtis. *An Outline of Government in Connecticut*, The Connecticut General Assembly, The House Committee on Public Information, 1949.

Davis, Jefferson B. "The Need for Regional Thinking," in *Connecticut Government*, The Institute of Public Service, University of Connecticut, Winter/Spring, vol. 41, no. 1, (1995): 2-4.

DeLuca, Louis C. "Why New Campaign Finance Laws? The System Already Works," *The Hartford Courant*, 22 October 1999, p. 15.

Dempsey, John. Address to the Convention, *Journal of the Constitutional Convention of Connecticut,* 1965, Hartford, CT: State of Connecticut, 1965, 7-8.

DePino, Chris. Chairman, Republican State Central Committee of Connecticut, Class Presentation, University of Connecticut, October 25, 1999.

Dillon, John F. *Commentaries on the Law of Municipal Corporations*, 5th Edition, Boston: Little, Brown 1911, I. Sec. 237.

Donelly, Paul. "Don't Rob Connecticut of a Congressman," *The Hartford Courant*, 3 January 2002, p. A11.

Douglas, Charles Henry. *The Government of the People of Connecticut,* Philadelphia: Eldredge and Brother, 1896.

Dove, Roger M. "America is Bereft of Political Leaders with Vision," *The Hartford Courant*, June 16, 1992. p. B9.

Duffy, Daniel. "Congressional and State Legislative Redistricting," Office of Legislative Research Report, The Connecticut General Assembly, *OLR Report 2000-R-0989*, October 20, 2000.

Elazar, Daniel. *American Federalism: A View From the States*, 2nd Edition, New York: Thomas Y. Crowell Company, 1972.

Erikson, Robert S., McIver, John P. and Wright, Gerald C. Jr. "State Political Culture and Public Opinion," *American Political Science Review,* 81 (1987): 797-813.

Ferree, Donald G. "The Reform Party Prophet?" *The Public Perspective,* August/September: (1999): 5-7.

Freedman, Judith. "Regionalism: A Local Decision," *Connecticut Government*, The Institute of Public Service, University of Connecticut. vol. 41, no. 1, Winter/Spring (1995): 1-2.

Gebelle, Shelly. "Connecticut's Spending Cap," Connecticut Voices for Children, June 21, 2000, *Connecticut Budget Choices*, produced by the Melville Charitable Trust, <www. Med.yale.edu/childstudy/ct/ctvoices.kidslink/kidslink2/finance/tax%20 and % 20 budget/code/shortspendingcap.pdf> (22 October 2002).

Gervickas, Vicki. "Keep Connecticut Competitive in the Global Economy," *Connstruction*, vol. 39, no. 4, Winter (2000): 21-24.

Grant, Charles S. *Democracy in the Connecticut Frontier Town of Kent*, New York: W.W. Norton & Company, Inc., 1972.

Green, Rick. "Gambling's Deepest Debts." *The Hartford Courant*, 11 March 2002, p. B1.

Halliburton, Warren J. *The People of Connecticut*, 1984, Connecticut Yankee Publications, Inc., Norwalk, CT.

Harr, Dan. "State's Delegation to Shrink," *The Hartford Courant*, 29 December 2000, p. A15.

Heffley, Dennis R. and Steven P. Lanza. "Driving More? Enjoying it Less?" *The Connecticut Economy*, vol. 7, no. 4, Fall, (1999): 4-5.

Herrnson, Paul S. and Faucheux, Ron. "Outside Looking In: Views of Third Party and Independent Candidates." *Campaigns and Elections*, August 1999, <http://www.bsos.umd.edu/gvpt/herrnson/art3.html> (27 October 2002).

Hill, George. *Handbook for Connecticut Boards of Finance*, Storrs, CT: The Institute of Public Service, University of Connecticut, 1992.

Hill, George. *Handbook for Connecticut Selectmen*, Storrs, CT: The Institute of Public Service, University of Connecticut, 1998.

Hill, George. *Connecticut Municipal Government*, The Institute of Public Service, University of Connecticut. 1998.

Horton, Wesley W. *The Connecticut State Constitution, A Reference Guide*, Westport, CT: Greenwood Press, 1993.

Jacklin, Michele. "Democrats Cleaned GOP Clocks Statewide." *The Hartford Courant*, 15 November 2000, p. A15.

Jackubowski, Jason. Written correspondence to the Author, June 22, 2002.

Jackson, Robert. "Hartford Democrats-Party of the People," *The Hartford Courant*, 27 October 1999, p. A17.

Janick, Herbert F. Jr. *A Diverse People: Connecticut 1914 to the Present*, Volume 5 in Series of Connecticut History, Chester: The Pequot Press, 1975.

Janicki, Mary M. "Background on Differences in Connecticut Primary Laws," Office of Legislative Research, Connecticut General Assembly *OLR Report 2002-R-0142*, 4 February 2002.

Jefferson, Thomas. Letter to Samual Kercheval, July 13, 1816 quoted in Mason, Alpheus. T. *Free Government in the Making*, 2nd Edition, New York: Oxford University Press, 1956, 372. Cited in Advisory Commission on Intergovernmental Relations, *Citizen Participation in the American Federal System*, Wayne F. Anderson, Executive Director, United States Government Printing Office, 1980.

Johnson, Richard B., Benjamin A. Trustman and Charles Y. Wadsworth, *Town Meeting Time*, Boston: Little Brown and Company, 1962.

Julien, Andrew. "State Files Suit Against Four HMOs," *The Hartford Courant*, 8 December 2000, p. A8.

Keating, Christopher. "House: Simmons, Johnson Win Key Congressional Races," *The Hartford Courant*, 6 November 2002, p. A1.

Keating, Christopher. "Senate Votes to Disband Sheriffs," *The Hartford Courant*, 13 April 2000, p. A3.

Keating, Christopher. " 'Filthy Five' Plants Prevail," *The Hartford Courant*, 27 April 2000, p. A18.

Klebanoff, Howard. "Legislative Oversight: The Neglected Legislative Function," in *Perspectives of a State Legislature*, edited by Clyde D. McKee, Jr., 95-103, Hartford: Hartford: Aetna Life and Casualty, 1978.

Kravchuk, Robert S. "The 'New Connecticut': Lowell Weicker and the Process of Administrative Reform," *Public Administration Review,* vol. 53, no. 4 July/August (1993): 329-339.

Lanza, Steven P. "The Ups and Downs of the Connecticut Income Tax," *The Connecticut Economy,* vol. 9, no. 2 Spring (2001):12-13.

Lasswell, Harold D. *Politics: Who Gets What, When, How,* New York: The World Publishing Co., 1963.

League of Women Voters of Connecticut. *How a Bill Becomes a Law in Connecticut,* (undated).

Lender, John and Mark Pazniokas. "3 Plead Guilty in Corruption Case," *The Hartford Courant,* 24 September 1999, p. A1.

Levenson, Rosaline. *County Government in Connecticut, Its History and Demise,* second printing, Storrs, CT: Institute of Public Service, University of Connecticut, 1981.

Lewis, Carol W. *Making Choices for Connecticut,* Storrs, CT: Institute of Public Service, University of Connecticut, 1984.

Lieberman, Joseph I. *The Legacy: Connecticut Politics 1930-1980,* Hartford: Spoonwood Press, 1981.

Lieberman, Joseph I. *The Power Broker: A Biography of John M. Bailey, Modern Political Boss,* Boston: Houghton Mifflin, 1966.

Lieberman, Joseph I., with Michael D'Orso. *In Praise of Public Life,* New York: Simon and Schuster, 2000.

Lieberman, Joseph. I. "Guidelines for Initiating Legislation and Understanding its Scope," in *Perspectives of a State Legislature,* edited by Clyde D. McKee, Jr., 53-62, Hartford: Aetna Life and Casualty, 1978.

Lightman, David. "Battle Over Soft Money is On," *The Hartford Courant,* 12 February 2002, p. A4.

Lockard, Duane. *New England State Politics.* Princeton: Princeton University Press, 1959.

Lorch, Robert L. *State and Local Politics,* Sixth Edition, Upper Saddle River: Prentice Hall, 2001.

Lyons, Moira. "Transportation: The Time to Start is Now." *The Connecticut Economy,* vol. 9, no. 2, Spring (2001): 20.

Mahony, Edmond H. "More Details on Giordano," *The Hartford Courant*, 19 September 2002, p. B1.

Maltbie, William M. "The First Constitution of Connecticut," Connecticut Secretary of the State, *Connecticut State Register and Manual*, 2001 Hartford, 2001, 56.

Marone, James A. *The Democratic Wish*, New York: Basic Books, 1990.

McEachern, Will. "Connecticut's Progressive Income Tax," *The Connecticut Economy*, vol. 6, no. 2 Spring, (1998):18-19.

McIntire, Mike and Jon Lender. "Silvester Staffers Landed State Jobs," *The Hartford Courant*, 14 November 1999, p. A13.

McKee, Clyde D. Jr. "Connecticut: A Political System in Transition," in *New England Political Parties*, edited by Josephine F. Milburn and William Doyle, 9-71, Cambridge, MA: Schenkman Publishing Company, Inc., 1983.

McKee, Clyde D. Jr. "Constitutional Principles and the Quest for Power," in Perspectives of a State Legislature, edited by Clyde D. McKee, Jr., 3-13, Hartford: Aetna Life and Casualty, 1978.

McKee, Clyde D., Jr. and Peterson, Paul. "Connecticut: Party Politics as a Steady Habit," in *Parties and Politics in the New England States*, ed. Jerome M. Mileur, 113-134, Polity Publications, Inc., Amherst, Massachusetts, 1997.

Merritt, Grace E. "Public Office Losing Luster," *The Hartford Courant*, 4 September 2001, p. B1.

Miringoff, Mark, William Hoynes, Sandra Opkycke and Marque-Luisa-Miringoff. *The Social State of Connecticut*, Tarrytown, New York: Fordham Institute for Innovation in Social Policy, 2001.

Moon, David C., Pierce, John C. and Lovrich, Nicholas. "Political Culture in the Urban West: Is it really Different?" *State and Local Government Review*, vol. 33, no. 3, (Fall 2001): 195-201.

Mooney, Thomas B. *A Practical Guide to Connecticut School Law*,, Second Edition, Wethersfield, CT: Connecticut Association of Boards of Education, Inc., 2000.

Morehouse, Sarah McCally. *State Politics, Parties and Policy*, New York: Holt, Rinehart and Winston, 1981.

Moy, Kimberly W. "New Map May Alter Political Futures," *The Hartford Courant*, 3 December, 2001, p. B3.

"Mr. Rowland's Phone Calls," *The Hartford Courant*, 5 October 2001, p. A12.

Murphy. Russell, D. "Connecticut: Lowell P. Weicker, Jr., a Maverick in the 'Land of Steady Habits'," in *Governors and Hard Times*, edited by Thad L. Beyle, 61-75, Congressional Quarterly Press, Washington, DC, 1992.

Norman-Eady, Sandra. Office of Legislative Research, Connecticut General Assembly, *OLR Report 93-r-00739*, 20 October 1993.

Ogle, David. "The Modernization of the General Assembly," in *Perspectives of a State Legislature*, edited by Clyde. D. McKee Jr., 17-31, Hartford: The Aetna Life and Casualty Company, 1978.

Osborn, Morris Galpin, editor. *History of Connecticut*, vols. 1 and 2, New York: The States History Company, 1925.

Pazniokas, Mark and Janice D'arcy. "Wine, Gems and Cash," The *Hartford Courant*, 1 November 2001, p. A1.

Permanent Commission on the Status of Women. 2000 Annual Report. *Women of the New Millennium*, 2000.

Porth Richard J. "Our Commonweal," *Connecticut Government*, vol. 42, no. 1, Institute of Public Service, University of Connecticut. Winter/Spring (1997): 6-8.

Purmont, Jon. E. "20 Years Later, We Remember Ella Grasso," *The Hartford Courant*, 5 February 2001, p. A9.

Quinnipiac College Poll. "Patriots Deal Sacks Rowland's Approval, Connecticut Voters Reject Deal Before Team Pulls Out," Doug Schwartz, Poll Director, <http://www.quinnipiac.edu/polls/> (Release 4 May 1999).

Quinnipiac College Poll. "Generation X-ers Show Lower Interest in Politics than Boomers and Mature Generations," Doug Schwartz, Poll Director. <http://www.quinnipiac.edu./polls/> (Release 26 October 1999).

Ranney, Austin. "Parties in State Politics," in *Politics in the American States*, edited by Herbert Jacob and Kenneth N. Vines, Boston: Little, Brown, 1971.

Rappa, John. "History of Connecticut's Boroughs," Office of Legislative Research, Connecticut General Assembly, *OLR Report 98-R-0660*, 12 June 1998.

Reeher, Grant. *Narratives of Justice*, Ann Arbor: University of Michigan Press, 1996.

Reenie, Kevin F. "Connecticut Swayed a Convention 60 Years Ago," *The Hartford Courant*, July 28, 2000, p. A19.

Reubenbauer, Kathleen M. State of Connecticut, Office of Policy and Management, Presentation at the University of Connecticut, 58th Annual School for Assessors. 21 June 2002.

Richards, Margaret. *350 Years of Connecticut Government: A Search for the Common Good*, Journal Activities compiled by William Marcy, edited by Denise Wright Merrill, Connecticut Consortium for Law and Citizenship Education, Inc., Hartford, 1988.

Rose, Gary L. *Connecticut Politics at the Crossroads*, Lanham: University Press of America, Inc., 1992.

Roth, David M. *Connecticut: A Bicentennial History*, New York: W.W. Norton and Co. Inc, 1979.

Rowland, John G. Governor of Connecticut, Letter to Secretary of the State Susan Bysiewicz, 5 May 2000.

Sandel, Michael J. *Democracy's Discontent*, Cambridge: The Belknap Press of Harvard University Press, 1996.

Satter, Robert. *A Path in the Law*, Guilford, Connecticut: The Connecticut Law Book Company, 1996.

Sembor, Edward. C. "On Knowledge and Interest," *Connecticut Government*, vol. 42, no. 1, Institute of Public Service, University of Connecticut, Winter /Spring (1997): 1-2.

Sembor, Edward. C. "Building Community Citizenship Through Study Circles," *Public Management,* vol. 74, no. 6, June (1992): 15-17.

Shipman, Gene. Interview by Elissa Papirno, *The Hartford Courant,* 19 January 1992, C1, C4.

Shortall, Joseph M. Esq. and Carlow, Brian Esq. "Criminal and Juvenile Justice in Connecticut," in *Street Law: A Course in Practical Law,* Connecticut Supplement, 3rd Edition, Connecticut Bar Association: West Publishing Group, 1989.

Simsbury Town Manager Study Committee. *Report to the Board of Selectman*, April, 1997.

Stamps, Norman LeVaun. *Political Parties in Connecticut*, 1789-1819, Ph.D. Dissertation, Yale University, Political Science, New Haven: Yale University, 1968.

Stannard, Charles. "Redrawn Districts Swap Some Voters," *The Hartford Courant*, (Shoreline-Greater New Haven Edition) 3 December 2001, p. B3.

Stuart, Patricia. The Connecticut Town Meeting, Storrs, CT: The Institute of Public Service, University of Connecticut, 1984.

Swan, Tom. "What a Bargain!" *The Hartford Courant*, 4 March 2001, p. C1.

Swanson, Wayne R. *Lawmaking in Connecticut: The General Assembly*, New London, CT: Wayne R. Swanson, 1978.

Swift, Mike, "Poverty's Web Widens," *The Hartford Courant*, 24 May 2002, p. B3.

Swift, Mike and Tom Puleo. "Two Egos, One Mess," *The Hartford Courant*, 13 June 1999, p. A12.

Thompson, Joel A. and Gary F. Moncrief. *Campaign Finance in State Legislative Elections*, Washington, DC, Congressional Quarterly Inc., 1998.

TIME. "10 Questions for Jesse Ventura," 29 April 2002: 8.

Trecker, Janice Law. *Preachers, Rebels, and Traders*, Connecticut 1818 to 1865, vol. 3, Series in Connecticut History, a publication of The Center for Connecticut Studies, Eastern Connecticut State College, Chester: The Pequot Press, 1975.

Trumbull, J. Hammond. *Historical Notes on the Constitutions of Connecticut, 1639-1818*, Hartford, CT: The Case, Lockwood and Brainard Company, 1901.

Webster, Noah. "A Brief History of Political Parties in the United States," in A Collection of Papers on Political, Literary and Moral Subjects, New York: Webster and Clark, 1843, Chapter XIX.

United States Bureau of the Census. "State Government Employment Data, Connecticut State Government, March 2000," Washington, D.C. <http://blue.census.gov/govs/apes/00stct.txt > (5 October 2002).

United States Bureau of the Census. Census 2000 Redistricting Data, (Public Law 94-171), Summary File, "Connecticut-Place and County

Subdivision," Geographic Comparison Table," Washington, DC, <http://factfinder.census.gov/bfb/_lang=en_vt_name=DEC-2000_PL_U_GCTPL_geo_id=04000US09.htm> (20 April 2002).

United States Federal Election Commission. "Campaign Finance Law 98: A Summary of State Campaign Finance Laws with Quick Reference Charts," Edward D. Feigenbaum, J.D. and James A. Palmer, J.D. <http://www.fec.gov/pages/cflaw98.htm> (30 September 2002).

Van Dusen, Albert. E. *Connecticut*, New York: Random House, 1961.

Van Dusen, Albert E. *Puritans Against the Wilderness: Connecticut History to 1763*, Volume 1 of the Series in Connecticut History. The Center for Connecticut Studies, Eastern Connecticut State College, Chester, CT: The Pequot Press, 1975.

White, Max R. "The Office of Selectman," in George E. Hill, *Handbook for Connecticut Selectman*, Storrs, CT: The Institute of Public Service, University of Connecticut, 1998.

Wirt, Clay L. "Dillon's Rule," *Virginia Town and City*, August, (1989):12-13.

Wright, Arthur W. "On This Roll of the Dice, Southeastern Connecticut (and the rest of us) Got Lucky," *The Connecticut Economy*, vol. 9, no. 1, Winter (2001): 12-13.

Zarem, Jane E., editor and compiler. *The Connecticut Citizen's Handbook, A guide to State Government*, Third edition, League of Women Voters of Connecticut Education Fund, Chester, CT: The Globe Pequot Press, 1987.

Court Cases

Town of Orange v. Modern Cigarette, Inc., 256 Conn. 557 (2001).

Leydon v. Greenwich, 257 Conn. 318 (2001).

Sheff v. O'Neil, 45 Conn. Sup. 630 (Superior Court, 3 March 1999).

Sheff v. O'Neil, 238 Conn. 1 (1996).

Charles v. Charles, 243 Conn. 255 (1997).

State v. Troupe, 237 Conn. 284 (1996).

Tashjian v. Connecticut, 479 U.S. 20, (1986).

Shelton v. Commissioner of the Department of Environmental Protection, 193 Conn. 506, 520-523 (1984).

Horton v. Meskill, 172 Conn. 615 (1977).

Westberry v. Sanders, 376 U.S. 1 (1964).

Reynolds v. Simms, 377 U.S. 533 (1964).

Butterworth v. Dempsey, 237 F. Supp. 302 (D. Conn.); 378 U.S. 564 (1964).

Gray v. Sanders, 372 U.S. 368, 381 (1963).

Baker v. Carr, 369 U.S. 186 (1962).

Worcester v. Worcester Consolidated Railway Company, 196 U.S. 539 (1905).

State Ex. Rel. Bulkeley v. Williams, (86 Conn. 131, 1896).

City of Clinton v. Cedar Rapids and Missouri River Rail Road Company, (24 Iowa, 455, (1868).

Willimantic School Society v. First School Society in Windham, 14 Conn. 457 (1841).

Willard v. Warden, 8 Conn. 247 (1830).

INDEX

Joint Reapportionment Committee, 2
judicial districts, 71
Judicial Selection Commission, 75

K

Kraft, Robert, 62, 64

L

Lasswell, Harold, 2
Latino and Puerto Rican Affairs
  Commission, 49
League of Women Voters of
  Connecticut, 113
legislative commissions, 48-49
legislative committees, 44
Leydon v. Greenwich, 77
Lieberman, Joseph, 36, 41
Lobbies, 49-52
Lockard, Duane, 1
Ludlow, Roger, 14

M

major political party, defined, 33, 35
Malloy, Dannel P., 95
Maltbie, William M., 16
Manager-council form, 95-97
March Commission, 13-14
Mashantucket Pequots, 7, 58
Massachusetts Bay Colony, 13
mayor-council form, 92-95
mayor, strong form, 93-95
mayor, weak form, 93-95
McKee, Clyde D., Jr., 12, 32
metropolitan planning organization
  (MPO), 108
Meskill, Thomas, 60
minimum expenditure requirement
  (MER), 25

minor political party, defined, 38-39
misdemeanors, 73
Missouri Plan, 75
Moorehouse, Sarah McCally, 27
Mohegan Sun Casino, 7
Moynihan, Timothy J., 54
municipal powers, 84-87
New England Patriots, 62-63

O

Office of the Auditors of Public
  Accounts, 48-49
Office of Fiscal Analysis, 45
Office of Legislative Research, 45
Office of Policy and Management, 57

P

parks, state, 6
Particular Court, 69-70
Pattyson, Meghan, 51-52
Permanent Commission on the Status
  of Women, 48
planning commission, 100
political culture, 9-10
political action committee, (PAC), 37
political parties, 28-34
primary election, 34
property tax, 97-98
probate court, 70-71
public safety, 100-101
Puritans, 13, 17

R

Ranney, Austin, 31
Ranney Index, 31
Rapoport, Miles, 111
Reeher, Grant, 45
redistricting, 2-3

reapportionment, 2-3
Reapportionment Commission, 2
regionalism, 107-110
regional planning agency (RPA), 108
Republican Party, 28-29
Reynolds v. Simms, 22
representative town meeting (RTM),
    92
revaluation, 98
Ribicoff, Abraham, 30, 60
Rome, Frankel and Kennelly, 50
Roraback, J. Henry, 29
Rose, Gary, 32
Rowland, John, 59, 60-65
Roy and LeRoy, 51

S

Satter, Robert, 49
Scheinblum, Howard, 74
Secretary of the State, 67, 111-112,
    116
selectmen, board of, form of
    government, 89-92
Sheff v. O'Neil, 25
Shelton v. Commissioner of the
    Department of Environmental
    Protection, 84
sheriff, 9
Silvester, Paul J., 8-9
soft money in campaigns, 38
special districts, 101
spending cap, 57-58
Stamps, Norman, 27-28
stand-up law, 20
state income tax, 4
State v. Troupe, 77
State Ex. Rel. v. Williams, 82
Study Circles Resource Center, 114-
    115
Superior Court, 71-74
Supreme Court, 75

T

Tashjian v. Connecticut, 35
taxation in Connecticut, 4
tax collector, 99
tax assessor, 97-98
Terrorism, 64-65
Tenzer, Morton, 65
Toleration Ticket, 19
Town of Orange v. Modern
    Cigarette, Inc., 78
town meeting, 90-92
transportation, 5-6
Treasurer, Connecticut State, 61-62, 66

V

Van Dusen, Albert E., 16
Ventura, Jessie, 38-39
veto, 63-64

W

War of 1812, 19
Webster, Noah, 27
Westberry v. Sanders, 22
Weicker, Lowell P. Jr., 4, 33, 53, 55,
    58
Willard v. Warden, 82
Willimantic School Society v. First
    School Society in Windham, 82
Winthrop, John, 17
Wolcott, Oliver, 19
Worcester v. Worcester Consolidated
    Railway Company, 82

BIOGRAPHIC STATEMENT

Edward C. Sembor, Ph.D.

Dr. Edward Sembor has served as Associate Extension Professor at the Institute of Public Service, College of Continuing Studies, University of Connecticut since 1990 where he has developed non-credit educational programs serving the specific needs of state and local government officials. He has presented workshops on local budgeting, leadership and diversity training, has acted as facilitator for government and civic groups and has developed training programs with such groups as assessors, boards of assessment appeals, and town clerks throughout Connecticut. He also served in a joint appointment as assistant professor of political science at the university's Political Science Department where he has taught courses in public administration, state and local government and American government. His published work has appeared in *Public Administration Quarterly, Public Management, Social Education, The Hartford Courant* and *The New Haven Register*. He has been a featured presentor in civic education programs in Kaohsiung, Republic of China and Trakai, Lithuania. Before coming to the University of Connecticut, Dr. Sembor worked at the Office of Management and Budget, New York City under Mayor Edward Koch and at the Department of Administrative Services, Town of West Hartford, Connecticut. He was also vice-principal at East Catholic High School. He received his Ph.D. in political science from Fordham University. Dr. Sembor resides in Pomfret Center, Connecticut, with his wife and two daughters. He is a former member and chairman of the Pomfret Board of Education.